# Guide to Phrasing
# in Pitman New Era
# Shorthand

# Guide to Phrasing
# in Pitman New Era
# Shorthand

**June Swann,** MISW, FSCT, FIPS
lately Official Court Reporter
at the Central Criminal Court, London

Based on

## The New Phonographic Phrase Book

by

**Emily D. Smith,** B.Sc.(Econ.), F.R.S.A.

PITMAN

PITMAN PUBLISHING LIMITED
39 Parker Street, London WC2B 5PB

*Associated Companies*
Copp Clark Pitman, Toronto
Fearon-Pitman Publishers Inc, San Francisco
Pitman Publishing New Zealand Ltd, Wellington
Pitman Publishing Pty Ltd, Melbourne

*First published* 1975
*Reprinted* 1979

*Isaac Pitman*

Text set in 10/11 pt. Monotype Plantin, printed by photolithography,
and bound in Great Britain at The Pitman Press, Bath

ISBN 0 273 00707 6

(G9—672:24)

# Contents

vii

# Foreword

There are undoubtedly still some people who have the strange notion that, in order to reach shorthand speeds of 200 wpm and over, it is necessary to employ extreme short-cuts. In fact, it is probable that greater progress will result from the study and application of the rules for simple joining than will be experienced from the use of innumerable short-cuts. Consider for a moment one very small part of the vast 'principle of simple joining'—*tick the*. Next, look at any paragraph in any newspaper, magazine or book. The chances are that there will be several opportunities for joining *tick the*; the possibility of finding even one acceptable high-speed short-cut is remote indeed.

This book, therefore, deals with the *principles* of phrasing. It would be quite wrong to say that the learning of individual phrases is a waste of time; but, bearing in mind the frequency of some words in combination, it is much more productive to study, for example, the use of *pr* halved for *part* than to drill the single phrase ⟨shorthand symbol⟩ *all parts of the world*. In order to understand the principles completely, there must be some drilling of examples. The purpose of the drilling is to absorb the principle; the knowledge gained of the phrases used in the drill is a bonus.

The learning of the principles of phrasing may be likened to the special tickets that have from time to time been popular on buses and trains, which offer unlimited travel and variable routes. The learning of individual phrases is, by comparison, as restricting as a day-return ticket.

It will be seen that the book is arranged in sections, each consisting of explanation, examples and practice material. That format was originated by Miss Emily Smith when preparing *The New Phonographic Phrase Book*. Since it is the most logical and effective arrangement, it has been retained here. The text, however, has been re-written; the examples have for the most part been re-arranged; and the practice passages, with a few exceptions, have also been changed.

I am happy to acknowledge the great amount of work and expertise from which I have myself benefited, both as a student and in preparing this book. I should also like to thank the teacher colleagues who have advised me on particular vocabularies in the specialist section.

---

In each section, the various aspects of a principle are explained and illustrated with examples. A list of phrases including some of those used in the text follows; then there are passages of connected matter designed to practise the particular principle. The text of each section should be read thoroughly before going on to the Selected Phrases or Practice Material. Here are some suggestions for using them.

**Selected Phrases (in shorthand)**

(a) Though the examples have not been presented in the form of a facility drill, that does not preclude their use in such a way. One group of phrases should be dealt with at a time, the first copy being made carefully, and on subsequent lines the effort being directed to retaining the quality of the shorthand but increasing the speed of writing.

(b) Individual outlines may be drilled for a quarter of a minute. Some time should be spent practising the particular phrase beforehand so that there is no hesitation in the writing. The quarter-minute should be timed (preferably by someone else) and afterwards the words per minute calculated. That is done by counting the number of times the phrase has been written, multiplying by four, then multiplying by the number of words in the phrase. For example, ........ *paid up capital of the company* written 15 times in the quarter-minute $= 15 \times 4 \times 6$, i.e. 360 wpm.

(c) A complete set of Selected Phrases may be used as a timed reading exercise. The first time the phrases are read, the time taken should be noted. On the second and third readings, every effort should be made to reduce the time. (If more than three such attempts are made, boredom may prevent any further increase in the speed of reading.)

(d) The same phrases may be used as a test of the writer's understanding of the principle dealt with in a particular section. First of all, the examples might be transcribed into longhand from the shorthand (the results should be carefully checked); then, from the longhand, a shorthand copy might be prepared. At the end of the writing, it is important to check the accuracy of the work and to drill any corrections. (*Note*. At all times the principle that is being practised should be kept well in mind.)

## Practice Material

(i) *Shorthand*

(a) These passages may be used as fair-copying exercises to improve penmanship.

(b) They may be fair-copied, leaving a blank line or lines after each line of shorthand, and then used as a facility drill.

(c) Timed reading is also a useful exercise; and with these passages, which are elsewhere counted in tens, the exact speed of reading may be determined.

(d) The shorthand copy may be compared with a writer's own notes taken from dictation, in order to assess what remedial work, if any, is necessary.

(*Note*. In order to be fully effective, timed reading exercises are best read aloud.)

(ii) *Longhand*

(a) This material is counted in tens and may therefore be used as straightforward dictation material.

(b) It may be used as a key if a typewritten (or handwritten) transcript is prepared from the shorthand copy.

(c) All the phrases (which are indicated by means of hyphens)—not only those employing a particular principle—may be extracted from the passage prior to dictation and used as a facility drill.

---

It is difficult for us to realize that shorthand phrasing had to be "invented". There was a time when *in the course of his speech* would

have been rendered by the single outlines: ⌣ . ᴄᵗᵒ ᴼ ᵍ .

Students had to learn to progress from that primitive and time-wasting

effort to ⌣ ᴄᵗᵒ ᵍ and, at a later stage, to ᴬᵍ . So writers

today need to study the *principles* of phrasing and practise them by means of examples and specially prepared material containing the appropriate expressions.

Any passage that has been designed to include more than its fair share of phrases dealing with, for example, omission of *con-* is bound to be a little artificial. Occasionally, it is also necessary to bend the rules of English grammar a little. Though every effort has been made to avoid blatant errors, one word of warning: a practice passage may be headed "Memo to . . .", but the language in style and quality is not intended to be a model. To that warning may be added another: the same less-than-perfect language is, unfortunately, encountered in everyday speech. So, though it may be realistic, do not be tempted to imitate it.

Throughout, a full knowledge of shorthand theory has been assumed; and it should not be thought, because a section is headed *Circle s*, that nothing more advanced than *Circle s* is included. To adopt such an arrangement would be too limiting.

---

A study of the contents of this book, consolidated by the appropriate practice, should enable almost anyone to achieve an increased speed of writing. If the principles have been thoroughly mastered, they may be extended or adapted to the particular needs of individual writers.

JUNE SWANN

# PART ONE

## General Principles

The general approach to phrasing is the same as that to any other part of the Pitman shorthand system. There are three overriding principles: that the form should be

(1) easy to write (principle of facility);
(2) within reasonable limits above or below the line (principle of lineality);
(3) capable of quick recognition (principle of legibility).

In addition, as with word-outlines (where considerations such as vowel indication may be concerned), there are one or two other points that should be borne in mind:

(4) although the first outline always keeps its own position, certain outlines may be raised or lowered to allow other joined outlines also to remain in their own position;
(5) phrases should be devised for commonly recurring groups or ones that would otherwise be excessively difficult to write;
(6) the sense of what has been taken down may be suggested by the grouping of words into phrases.

# Section I

## *General; Simple Joining; Position of First Outline*

### 1 Principle of facility

If a phrase is not easy to write, it is hardly worth while using it, for the interruption in the flow of writing will cancel out the time saved by the joining. Some writers appear determined to phrase anything with even a hint of a favourable join, resulting in "fun" phrases like the following:

Such a phrase cannot be considered seriously for several obvious reasons. First, it runs down through a few writing-lines and is therefore likely to interfere with other material on those lines. Secondly, it may well be that the effort spent in producing such a complex form will leave the writer mentally exhausted and unable to continue recording accurately the rest of the passage. Thirdly, outlines should not be joined simply for the sake of it; there should be some positive benefit to be gained. Suggested phrasing:

Transcription: We shall be glad if you will please let us know if you are going to be present at the next annual general meeting.

## 2 Principle of lineality

Just as the phrase in (1) descends too far below the line (and therefore, as has been said, breaks the rule of lineality), it is possible to rise too far above the line. Again, to give an extreme example:

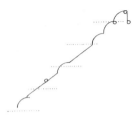

All the remarks made in (1) apply with equal force to that phrase; but here there is a further difficulty—the words, though physically easy to join, are not in a combination that would be written often. It might be splendid to write it, but there would be great difficulty in transcription, since it is not at once apparent where one word ends and another begins. Suggested representation:

Transcription: Lawyers really rarely lose law suits.


## 3 Principle of legibility

Phrasing is intended as an aid, not an obligation. If phrases cannot at once be recognized and read back, they cannot be "good" phrases. Most outlines of this sort offend against fundamental rules that are applied to word-outlines, such as not joining strokes of unequal length unless there is an angle. For example, ⌐ *I did do it* might, at the time of hearing the words, have seemed a good combination to phrase. When looked at written neatly on the page (let alone if slightly distorted in the hurry of recording a rapid speaker), it is shown up for what it is: a thoroughly bad phrase, no matter how easy it might have been to write, because it is not easily transcribed.

All such combinations of straight strokes, whether they break the basic rules of halving or not, are rarely successful; and phrases such as ＼ for *Bye, bye, Bobby* and ‿ for *I can kick Kate* are not acceptable or sensible.

4

The joining of the short form *and* sometimes leads to confusion. It is generally not safe to join it to simple straight strokes, as the only result is to make the stroke appear to be hooked. Curves will normally follow it quite well, but in some cases (for instance, before *m*) the two strokes simply merge and become shapeless and unreadable. These remarks apply to similar combinations, such as *to know, and are*.

Clarity is essential.

## 4 Raising and lowering of outlines

When outlines are joined together, the first outline is written in its own position, and any following outlines are simply joined on. This means that often the following word or words are out of position—e.g. *take up* . Sometimes, purely by chance, the following outlines will remain in their own position: *I am glad that* . If, however, the phrase is extended to read *I am glad that you can* , there is now a mixture of positions. In each case, though, it is the *first* word of the phrase that has determined the position.

There are a few occasions (usually with short forms) when the general principle explained above may be extended. The first outline in the phrase is still written above the line, but its position is marginally raised or lowered. By doing so, a following outline may also retain its own position—

| | | | |
|---|---|---|---|
| with much | | in those |
| with which | | in this |
| with each | | in these |

It is important to emphasize that the position of the first outline, although it has been adjusted slightly above or below the normal, is still clearly above the line in each of the examples.

## 5 Commonly recurring groups

It is obviously pointless to create principles of phrasing or individual phrases for combinations that are unlikely to occur very often. The phrase shown in (2) and those shown in the second paragraph of (3) are examples of such phrases. Be they good or bad in structure, the chances of having to write them (either with the words in the order shown, or at all) are so small that it is not worth devising a phrase to cover the group of words, nor designing a principle that would make them acceptable.

Also, what is useful to one writer may be of no value to another. In section 19 various suggestions are made to help writers in specialized fields apply certain *principles* to their own work.

## 6 Grouping according to sense

(a) The words *David said his sister had recently been abroad* may have two meanings. The first (as shown) implies that David is the one who is speaking and his sister is the one who has been abroad. If commas are put round *said his sister*, the meaning is reversed: the sister is the speaker, and David is the one who has been abroad. (Shorthand phrasing: )

It is unusual to insert punctuation other than full stops in shorthand notes. However, it is possible sometimes to show the speaker's meaning by the way in which the phrases are grouped. This is quite clearly seen if you compare (*I do not know*) and (*I do not, no*). In the first case, the phrase indicates that all the words occur together. In the second case, the comma in the longhand may be inferred from the separation in the shorthand.

The use and non-use of *tick the* provide further examples of implied speech patterns. In print, the following sentence would appear like this: *It was, the doctor said, the worst case of its kind that he had seen.* In the writer's notebook, it should appear as follows: If the tick is joined , the writer would, almost automatically, transcribe the words *It was the doctor . . .* before realizing that the words *the doctor said* were intended to be parenthetical.

Shorthand writers are constantly (and wisely) being urged to phrase, particularly to join *tick the* rather than use the dot and possibly confuse it with *a*; but the phrases must, if they are to be of more than academic value, reflect the sense of the words being recorded.

(b) In much the same way as punctuation may be indicated, emphasis on a particular word may be implicit in the written note. For instance, a person may be asked: *What was your address at that time?* If the answer

6

takes the form of the current address, the next question might be: *What* was *your address?* In the first case, the first four words of the shorthand would be as follows: ) ⌐ ↆ? In the second case, the shorthand could reflect the tone of voice in this way: ‿ ) ⌐ ↆ?

Consider the scope of different meanings possible here—

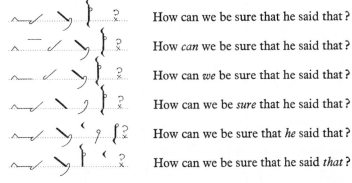

How can we be sure that he said that?

How *can* we be sure that he said that?

How can *we* be sure that he said that?

How can we be *sure* that he said that?

How can we be sure that *he* said that?

How can we be sure that he said *that*?

It is, therefore, apparent that phrasing can be more than just the simple joining together of outlines to save time-wasting pen-lifts. It can be a definite aid to transcription.

Other methods of distinction between pairs of possible transcription hazards are described in some detail in section 17. One such method is by vocalization; but, usually, unless there is some conflict, vowels should not be necessary in phrases.

As explained in the Foreword, each section concludes with a selection of outlines and a number of practice passages, so that the principles explained may be fully understood and developed. In the case of simple joining, it will be realized that the selection of phrases must be very limited, since an exhaustive list of all possible combinations is not practical.

# Selected Phrases 1

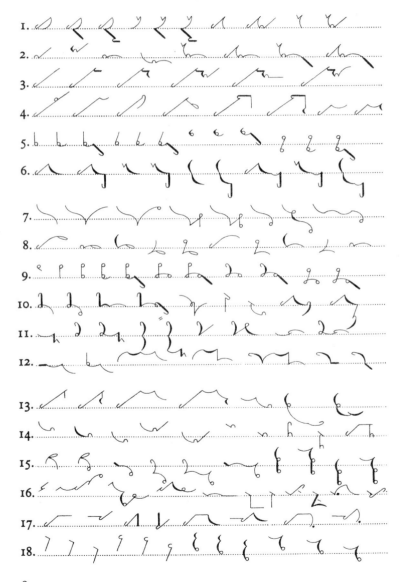

# Practice Material 1

(a)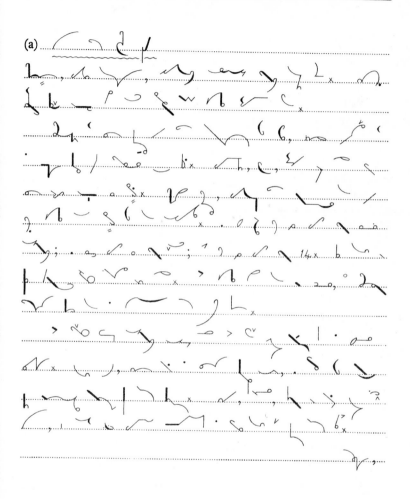

(b)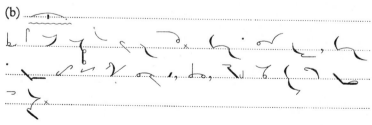

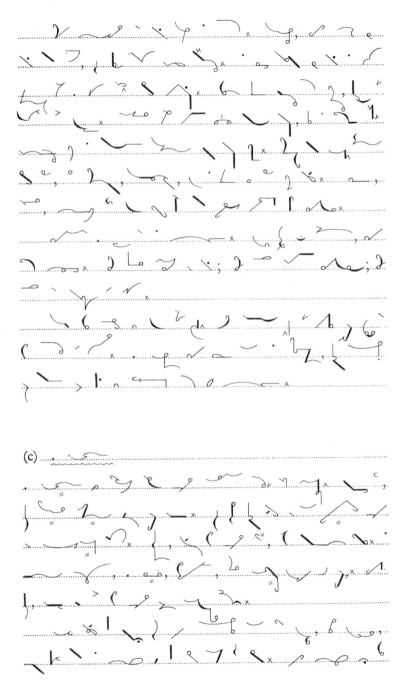

(c)

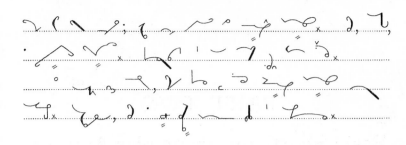

# PART TWO

## Basic Shorthand Principles Applied

## to Phrasing

The sections in Part Two show how the basic principles of Pitman shorthand can be applied to great advantage to shorten the outlines for many phrases. Instead of simply joining two outlines together, or raising or lowering an outline, the phrases in this Part cover the use of circles, loops and hooks, halving and doubling, and other principles. Writers are, therefore, applying to another field knowledge they have already gained. For instance, by the use of halving and doubling, instead of a final consonant (*t* or *d*) or a final syllable (*tr*, *dr*, *THr*) being added, whole words may be represented (*it*, *there*).

It is obviously necessary to practise the principles shown here as much as possible (preferably from dictation) by using the material provided. If a writer wishes to extend the application of any individual principle, it is vital to remember the three overriding factors (facility, lineality and legibility) and any specific points that are mentioned in the particular section.

Although the principle of omission is dealt with fully in section 16, it is seen also in earlier sections—notably section 15.

# Section 2

## *Tick The; Diphthongs; He*

### 1 Tick the

The word *the* has already been mentioned in section 1(6) of Part One. The points made here are not intended to conflict with what has gone before, but merely to set out the circumstances in which *tick the* may be joined (without interfering with the sense) in order to save time.

Although the short form for *the* is very short—reflecting how often the word itself is used—the tick is even faster to write, because it saves

breaking the flow of the writing. So that, instead of ⌣⋯. for *in the*, a

quicker representation is ⌣⁻. The second form is also less liable to be misread. When the dot is used, it is sometimes written indeterminately somewhere halfway between first and second position, leaving considerable doubt in some cases as to which word is intended. More-

over, further outlines may be attached to the tick—so that ⌣⁻

might become ⌣ₒ *in the case*, or ⌣ₑ *in the case of*—and in this way even more time can be saved.

*Tick the* should be used as often as possible, bearing in mind what has been said about natural grouping of words and also the points that follow.

(a) The tick may be written upwards or downwards, but its angle

never changes: it is the same as that of stroke *chay* /. This can

make a vital difference if the following outlines are compared: ⌣⌐

*know the* with ⌣ *now*; ⌐⋯ *as the* with ⌐ *as to*.

(b) Deciding which way to write the tick is really a matter of common sense. It is written upwards or downwards (remembering that the slope remains the same), whichever direction provides the sharper angle and therefore the clearer joining.

These go down:

⟍ be the     ⟶ give the     ↓ does the     ( thank the

⌣ in the     ⟶ to the     ⌐ should the     ⟍ ban the

Compare these, which go up:

∟ at the     ⌒ allow the     ⋁ then the     ⟋ gave the

⌒ may the     ⟍ or the     ⟍ above the     ∟ do the

It is, therefore, apparent that the addition of a hook or circle may involve a change of direction of the tick. For example, in the second group, after *d* ( ∟ *do the*) the tick normally goes up; when a circle *s* is added ( ↓ *does the*), the tick must go down instead. Similarly, following *p* and *b*, for instance, it is usual to write the tick down ( ⟍ *be the*); but notice what happens when a final *v* hook is added ( ⟍ *above the*).

When the tick is joined to ⌐ *but* and ⌐ *on*, it is obvious that the upward form would make the sharper angle. Unfortunately, if the short forms were written in the normal way, there could be confusion with the signs ⌐ *eye/I* and ⌐ *why*. Therefore, the angle of the tick stays the same, but the short forms themselves take on a slight slope so that no such confusion can arise: ⌐ *but the*, ⌐ *on the*.

(c) As has already been seen above, the tick may be used medially: ⌐ *at the end*    ⌐ *discuss the matter*    ⌐ *in the words*

(d) The tick is not usually written to a half-length straight stroke standing alone without initial or final attachments— ⟍ *bid the*; but ⌒ *robbed the*, ⟍ *bend the*.

(e) The tick is not used following the small and large loops, nor after the *ns* and *nses* circles:

↓ *test the*         ⌒ *hunts the*

⌒ *master the*       ⌒ *rinses the*

(f) *Tick the* may never be used initially. (Like *and*, it might cause confusion with hooks; and it might, of course, itself be confused with *and*.)

.......... call the    *but*    .......... the call

.......... suit the    *but*    .......... the suit

.......... grip the    *but*    .......... the grip

(*Note. The* is often left out altogether in phrases. This aspect is dealt with in section 16.)


## 2 Diphthongs

The diphthongs *i* and *ū* are also used, of course, for the short forms *I/eye* and *you*. These basic signs join quite easily and are often used to make phrases:

.......... I had         .......... you will

.......... I think       .......... do you

.......... I have        .......... you may

Sometimes, however, it is not possible to join the signs just as they are, and slight changes have to be made:

(a) Diphthong *i* would, if written before some strokes, blend with them (as has been described already in relation to *and* in section 1(3) of Part One), and in those cases the second half of the diphthong—which would be lost anyway—is simply not written at all:

.......... I will        .......... I tried

.......... I promise     .......... I may

.......... I remember    .......... I refer

The same form is used before *k* and *g*, *w* and other hooked strokes to which the full diphthong does not join easily:

.......... I can         .......... I tell you

.......... I gave        .......... I would

.......... I believe     .......... I criticized

The full  ˅ …….  is used in all other cases—that is to say, where no advantage would be gained by contracting it:

……⌒……   I follow

……)……   I say

……𝗅……   I disagree

(b) Diphthong *ū* may be turned on its side at the end (and sometimes in the middle) of a phrase, if a better outline is achieved:

……⌐……   to take you      ……⌒……   let you have

……⌐……   to agree with you   ……⌒……   sending you the

……⌐……   to give you      ……³……   what you

……⟋……   are you        ……⌐……   can you

Although that is necessary in those and similar cases, there are many examples where the ordinary form joins quite easily:

……⅂……   in which you     ……⌣……   if you can

……⌐……   for you        ……⌐……   I am sure you

……⌒……   will you        ……⅂……   I can tell you

When *you* is the first word of the phrase, the diphthong must, of course, retain its own position and its usual form:

……⟋……   you are        ……⌐……   you can

……⌐……   you would       ……⌐……   you mean

(*Note.* Apart from simple joining, as in ……⌢…… *how the,* the diphthongs *oi* and *ow* are not used in phrases.)


## 3 He

There are two ways of writing *he.* There is the full form ……𝑦…… and the short form ……ı……  .

(a) The full stroke is used whenever *he* (i) stands alone and (ii) occurs at the beginning of a phrase:

……𝑦…… he       ……𝑦…… he is       ……𝑦…… he should be

16

(b) The short form may be used when the word *he* comes in the middle or at the end of a phrase. It must not be used standing alone or at the beginning of a phrase:

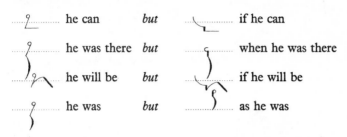

if he can ⟨ that he ⟩ as he ⟩ I know that he

Compare these pairs:

he can      *but*      if he can

he was there    *but*      when he was there

he will be      *but*      if he will be

he was      *but*      as he was

# Selected Phrases 2

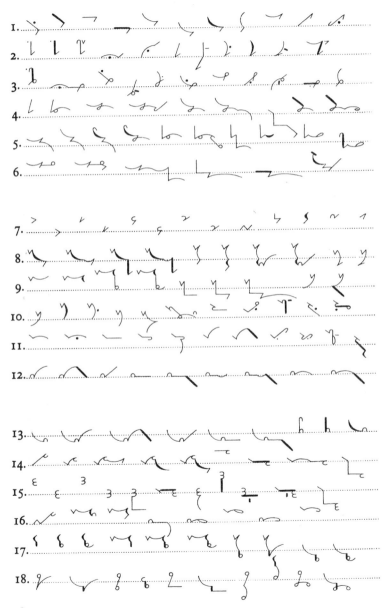

# Practice Material 2

(a)

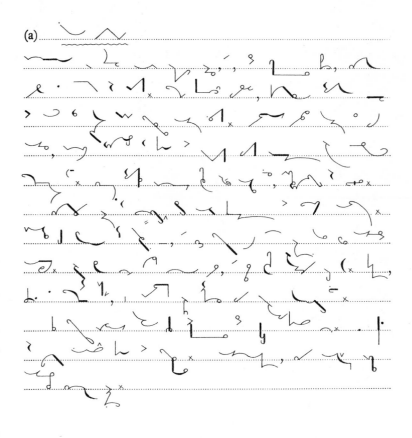

(b)

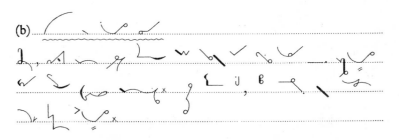

(c)

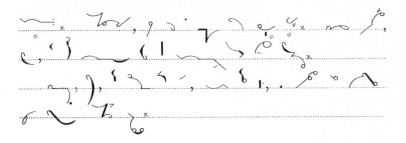

# Section 3

## Circle s

The small circle (which is, of course, used in the system to represent *s* at the beginning of a word and *s/z* medially or finally) is the short form for *is*, *his*, *as* and *has*. Even if it were limited to simple joining, therefore, it would have considerable phrasing potential. It may be used both in that and in the other ways explained below.

### 1 Simple circle

The small circle provides a fast and easy joining in many phrases:

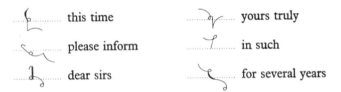

The normal direction of the circle is retained in the examples above.

In the same way, in such phrases as ⟨ *these matters*, ⟨ *this man*, the circle is written inside the first curve, and the *m* is written out from the stroke at the *top* of the circle. To try to do anything else would mean loss of facility and legibility—compare ⟨ *this kind*. There are, however, some cases where, in order to increase the opportunities for joinings, the direction of the circle is governed by the complete outline. For instance, compare the following:

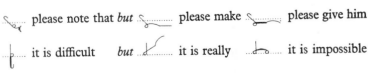

## 2 Is, his, as, has

The short form representing these four words can and should be used extensively:

| as | has | is | his |
|---|---|---|---|
| as it has not yet | it has | what is | in his opinion |
| as early as | it has been | is it | to his |
| as the | who has | it is mine | on his own |
| as to the | if he has | it is just as | by his |

(*Note.* The examples above have been listed under single headings. Some forms are, of course, capable of more than one combination—e.g. may be *it has* or *it is*.)

## 3 Us

The word *us* standing alone should be written in full with the stroke: . In phrases, the circle is a safe and rapid way to write it:

| | | | |
|---|---|---|---|
| tell us | | from us | |
| for us | | let us see | |
| to give us | | with us | |
| before us | | please let us know | |
| of us | | against us | |

## 4 Say

The simple word standing alone must, like *us*, be written in full: *say*. The use of the circle for this word in phrases should not be attempted until after the basic uses of circle *s* applied to phrasing have been mastered:

| | | | |
|---|---|---|---|
| we can say that | | to say a few words | |
| asked to say that | | I would like to say a few words | |

## 5 Once, n-us

The use of *ns* circle for *once* is, theoretically, limited to straight strokes. In fact, for practical purposes, there is only one combination that is likely to be used very much: ........ *at once.* (In most of the other cases where the *ns* circle would be possible, the stroke joins easily, and nothing would be gained by using the circle.) *At once* is such a common phrase that special treatment is justified. The circle on the *n* side may also represent *us* following *n:* ........ *upon us,* ........ *depend upon us.* (See also section 8(5), p. 55.)

## 6 Association

The combination *s-shun* makes a very short representation of the word *association,* as in:

........ political association     Automobile Association

........ consumers' association     legal association

## 7 As and r hook

The circle is closed on the *r* side to represent the word *as* in a phrase where the second word begins with a straight stroke, notably *p:*

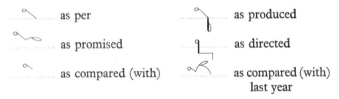

........ as per        as produced

........ as promised     as directed

........ as compared (with)     as compared (with) last year

## 8 Circle s and halving

A stroke that has been halved for the addition of *it* may take the circle following the halving:

........ if it is (has)       from its

........ if it is (has) not     in which it is (has)

The circle is read last—after the halving—in the usual way.

## 9 Circle s and doubling

The remarks above relating to halving apply equally to a stroke that has been doubled for the addition of *there*:

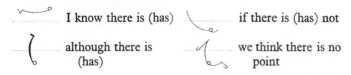

I know there is (has)    if there is (has) not

although there is (has)    we think there is no point

(*Note.* The principle explained in paragraph 5 may be extended to doubled strokes, as in: *to render us,* *hinder us.*)

## 10 Circle s instead of st loop

There are many quite common groups of words that include a medial *st*. In a large number of such cases the circle may be substituted for the loop, in order to make the joining possible:

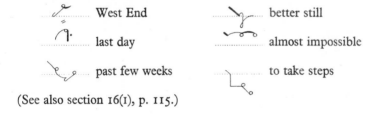

West End    better still

last day    almost impossible

past few weeks    to take steps

(See also section 16(1), p. 115.)

## 11 S followed by s or sw

Occasionally a final *s* of one word and an initial *s* of a following word are represented by a single circle, as *chairman's speech.*

More often when *s* is followed by another *s*, or sometimes *w*, the large circles *ss* and *sw* are used, as explained in section 4.

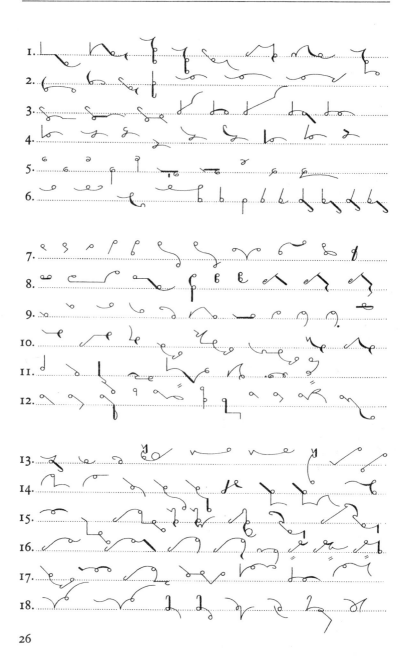

# Practice Material 3

(a) (i)

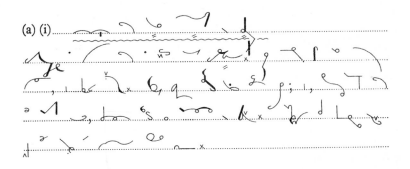

(ii)

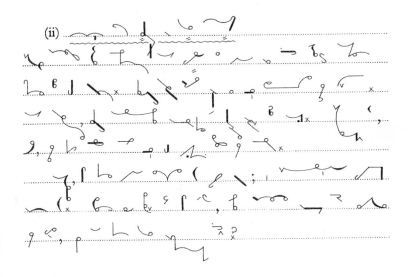

(iii)

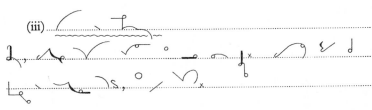

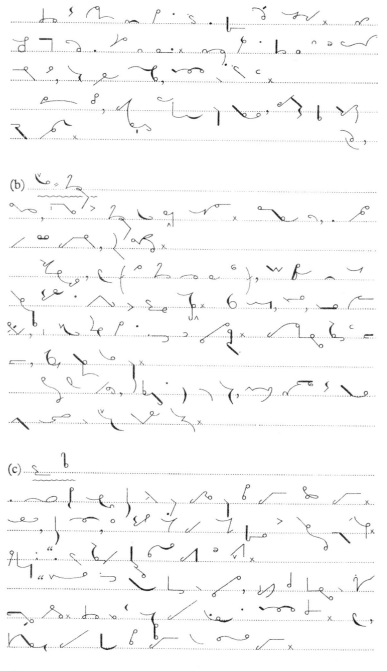

(b)

(c)

28

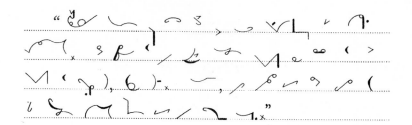

# Section 4

## *Circles Sw and Ss*

The large circles are used widely in phrases for all the many combinations of *s-w* and *s-s*. The various uses of the circles (initially, medially, finally or standing alone) are indicated below, the words and/or consonants represented being shown.

### 1 Initially

(a) *As we*

The most extensive initial use of the *sw* circle is in phrases beginning with the words *as we*. A number of examples are given here, but the principle should be employed whenever it is reasonable to do so within the limits of facility and legibility:

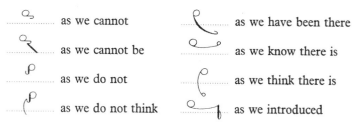

| | |
|---|---|
| as we can | as we are |
| as we can be | as we have |
| as we know that | as we feel |
| as we may | as we do |

An instance where an initial *as we* cannot be represented by the circle is ......... *as we went*. That would apply equally to any similarly hooked strokes—for instance, the *pl* group.

The *sw* circle may safely be written to a halved or doubled stroke:

| | |
|---|---|
| as we cannot | as we have been there |
| as we cannot be | as we know there is |
| as we do not | as we think there is |
| as we do not think | as we introduced |

Further phrases may be formed by closing the *sw* circle on the *r* side (in the same way as the small circle in section 3(7) was closed to represent *as*):

as we trust    as we promised    as we brought

(b) *As-w*

This use of *sw* circle initially is limited to a small but important group of phrases:

as will (well)          as well as

as will be              as well as possible

as will be seen         as well as can be

(See also section 13(3e), p. 89.)

(c) *As-s*

Although the *ss* circle is not normally used initially, it is acceptable at the beginning of a few very common phrases. This exceptional treatment is justified by the frequency with which the phrases are written and the fact that the outlines for them are clear and easy to write:

as soon as              as satisfactory as

as soon as possible     as suggested

as soon as we can       as said

## 2 Medially and finally

(a) *S-is* (*has*)

this is (has)           it is his

this has been           this is done

(b) *Is/has/his-s*

it is certain           there is something

there is some           for his sake

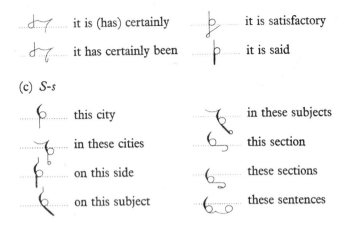

| | |
|---|---|
| it is (has) certainly | it is satisfactory |
| it has certainly been | it is said |

(c) *S-s*

| | |
|---|---|
| this city | in these subjects |
| in these cities | this section |
| on this side | these sections |
| on this subject | these sentences |

## 3 Standing alone

The large circle, depending upon its position, may represent any pair of the words *as, has, is, his*:

as is, as has, as his, has his

is as, is his, his is, his has

(*Note.* It is also possible to use the large circle in combination with other signs: *as is the*, *as has been*.)

# Selected Phrases 4

# Practice Material 4

(a)
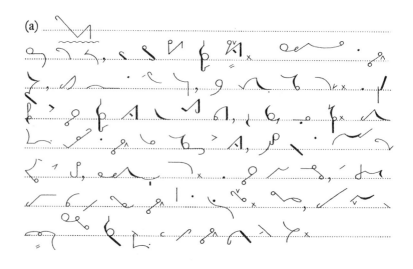

(b)

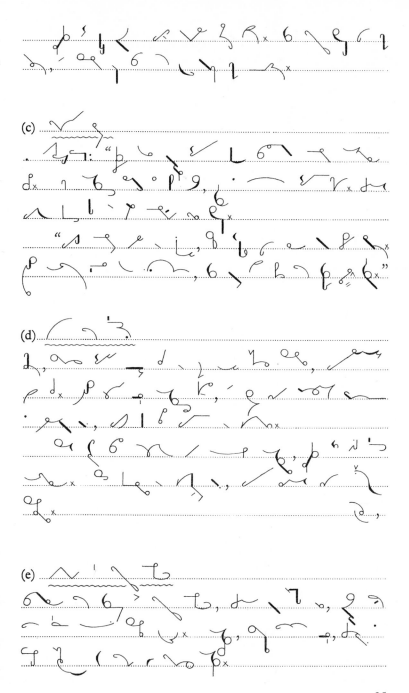

(c)

(d)

(e)

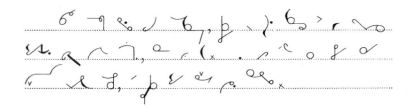

# Section 5

## St Loop

The small loop is used in phrases to represent the words *first* and *next*. It may also provide a link in phrases that involve simple joining.

### 1 Simple joining

(a) 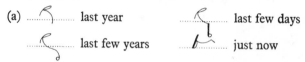 last year     last few days

last few years     just now

(b) Circle *s* for *as* or *us* follows the loop in the ordinary way:

as fast as     against us

### 2 First

When the word *first* comes at the beginning or in the middle of a phrase, the short form ⟋ is usually retained—though medially the loop is occasionally better. When *first* comes at the end of a phrase, the loop is always used.

In a few cases, neither link is satisfactory: e.g. ⟋ *first rate*, ⟋ *at first sight* (see also section 16(1a), p.115.)

(a) *Initially*

⟋ first time     ⟋ first place

⟋ first thing     ⟋ first class

⟋ first instance     ⟋ first-day cover

⟋ first-hand information     ⟋ first-aid

37

(b) *Medially*

.................... at first cost

.................... at first hand

.................... in the first place

.................... for the first time

.................... in the first instance

.................... in the first case

(c) *Finally*

.................... at first

.................... very first

## 3 Next

Just as the direction of the small circle is changed to include *n*, as explained in section 3, so the *st* loop is turned to the hook *n* side to add *next*:

.................... Sunday next

.................... Monday next

(See also section 8(6), p. 55.)

# Selected Phrases 5

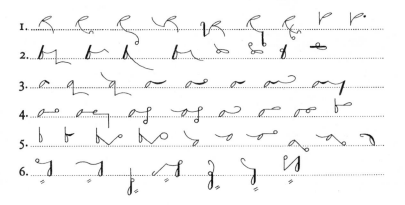

# Practice Material 5

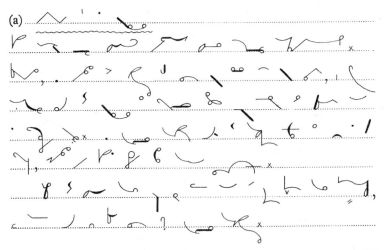

(b)

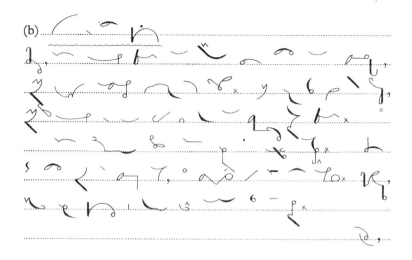

# Section 6

# R Hook

The *r* hook to both straight and curved strokes is used in phrases to shorten many words. By abbreviating the outlines

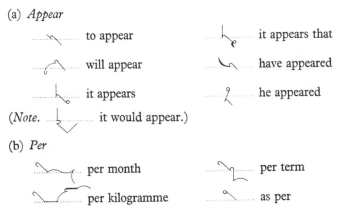

as shown in the following paragraphs, a better and faster joining is possible.

In some cases, the use of the hook enables a word that would not normally be capable of other than limited use in phrasing to be joined to a much greater extent.

Certain hooked forms are also used as intersections.

The use of the hooked forms is not restricted to the particular words included here. Advanced writers, especially if they are working in specialized vocabularies, may find it more helpful to adapt these suggestions to words that are more common in their own work—or, indeed, to extend them.

## 1 R hook to straight strokes

(a) *Appear*

  to appear     it appears that

  will appear     have appeared

  it appears     he appeared

(*Note.*   it would appear.)

(b) *Per*

  per month     per term

  per kilogramme     as per

The form ....⌄.... sometimes makes an easier joining than the hooked stroke, as in: ....⌄.... *per cent,* ....⌄.... *per annum,* ....⌄1.... *per head.* (See also section 13(1), p. 86.)

(c) *Park*

....⌐⌐.... Hyde Park  ....⌐⌐.... local park

....⌐⌐.... Central Park  ....⌐⌐.... car park

....⌐⌐.... Finsbury Park  ....⌐⌐.... Elm Park

(d) *Part*

The hooked form is used in combination with the halving principle to form phrases with *part*:

....⌐.... to take part  ....⌐.... in all parts of the country

....⌐.... major part  ....⌐.... part and parcel

....⌐.... in all parts  ....⌐.... for the most part

The full form is retained in ....⌄.... *part of* when the phrase stands by itself.

## 2 R hook to curves

(a) *Are*

The hooked form may be used in phrases where *are* follows *they*:

....)....  they are  ....)....  they are not

....)....  if they are  ....)....  that they are

In many other cases, of course, the short form ..../.... joins quite easily, e.g. ..../.... *how are,* ..../.... *we are.*

(b) *Our*

The hooked form may be used in phrases where *our* follows *in*:

....⌣.... in our  ....⌣.... in our opinion

....⌣.... in our country  ....⌣.... it is in our interests

42

As with *are,* the short form for *our*  is used in other cases, e.g. ⎯✓⎯ *to our,* ⎯✓⎯ *of our.*

## (c) *Order*

Doubling, in addition to the hook, is necessary to represent *order* following *in*:

⎯⎯⎯ in order                    ⎯⎯⎯ in order that

Halving is used in the following phrases:

⎯⎯⎯ in order to                    ⎯⎯⎯ in order to be sure

The full outline is used in other phrases, e.g. ⎯⎯⎯ *your order.*

(See also section 12(3b), p. 82.)

## (d) *Assure*

⎯⎯⎯ I can assure you                    ⎯⎯⎯ we are assured

⎯⎯⎯ to assure the                    ⎯⎯⎯ if you can assure us

## (e) *Far*

⎯⎯⎯ how far                    ⎯⎯⎯ by far the most

⎯⎯⎯ so far                    ⎯⎯⎯ by far the most important

⎯⎯⎯ very far                    ⎯⎯⎯ is it far

## (f) *Forth*

⎯⎯⎯ set forth                    ⎯⎯⎯ so forth

## 3 R hook and circle s

Occasionally, the final *r* hook at the beginning of one outline is closed to include a final circle *s* in a preceding outline:

⎯⎯⎯ it is agreed                    ⎯⎯⎯ purchase agreement

## 4 Intersections

The hooked forms *pr*, *spr* and *kr* make useful intersections as follows:

(a) *Professor*

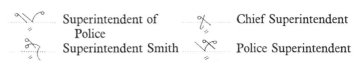

Professor of Music

Regius Professor

Professor Martin

French Professor

(b) *Superintendent*

Superintendent of Police

Chief Superintendent

Superintendent Smith

Police Superintendent

(c) *Colonel*

Colonel Jones

Lieut-Col Dean

Colonel Jackson

Lieut-Col Ball

(d) *Corporation*

corporation tax

finance corporations

corporation law

Steel Corporation

# Selected Phrases 6

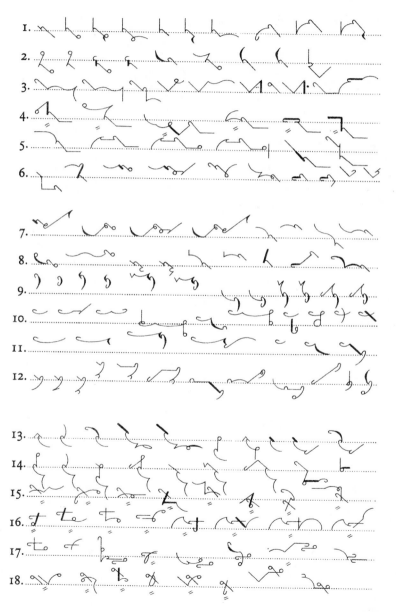

# Practice Material 6

(a)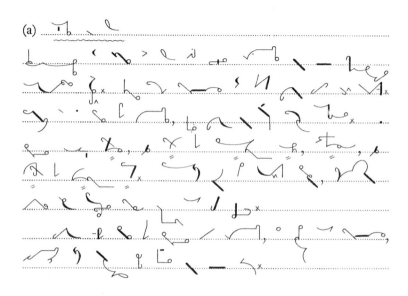

(b)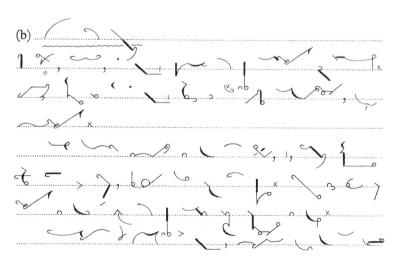

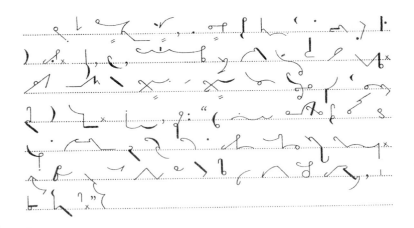

# Section 7

## L Hook

The *l* hook is used in phrases to represent the words *all*, *only* and *fellow*. The hooked form *pl* may be used as an intersection for *application*.

### 1 All

*L* hook is added to the straight strokes *t* and *b* in phrases beginning with the words *at all* and *by all*:

| | | | |
|---|---|---|---|
| | at all | | by all |
| | at all costs | | by all means |
| | at all events | | by all accounts |
| | at all times | | by all reports |

In other cases, such as ⌐ *in all* and ⌐ *for all*, simple joining of the basic forms is clearer than using the hook.

### 2 Only/fellow

The full forms ⌐ and ⌐ may be shortened in phrases to ⌐ and ⌐ .

(a) *Only*

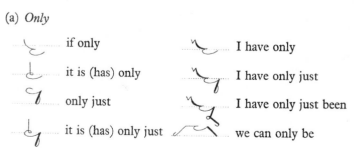

| | | | |
|---|---|---|---|
| | if only | | I have only |
| | it is (has) only | | I have only just |
| | only just | | I have only just been |
| | it is (has) only just | | we can only be |

_it will only_          _he may only_

_it will only be_          _he may only have_

Sometimes the full outline is both easier to write and clearer to read back—for instance, (i) when the word *only* stands alone; (ii) in phrases such as ⟨ ⟩ *only been*; (iii) when *only* follows *n* or a *straight* upstroke, as ⟨ ⟩ *you are only*.

(b) *Fellow*

fellow citizens          fellow students

fellow members          fellow directors

## 3 Application

The hooked form ⟨ ⟩ *pl* may be intersected to represent the word *application*, as in ⟨ ⟩ *to make application*, ⟨ ⟩ *written application*. (See also section 15(2), p. 107.)

# Selected Phrases 7

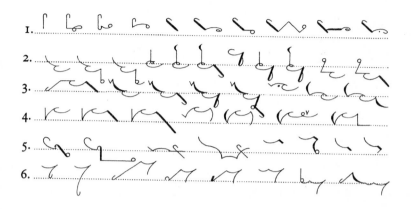

1.
2.
3.
4.
5.
6.

# Practice Material 7

(a)

(b)

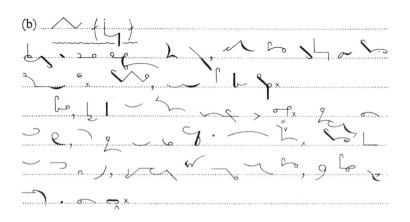

# Section 8

# N Hook

The *n* hook may be used in phrasing to represent the following words:

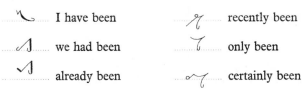

been    on    not    next

than    own    once

It is also used in the intersections for *beginning* and *convenient/ce*.

The principles of phrasing explained here may, like most other principles, be adapted or extended to suit the needs of individual writers.

## 1 Simple addition of n hook

(a) *Been*

I have been    recently been

we had been    only been

already been    certainly been

(*Note.* When *been* follows stroke *n*, another hook or a circle, the hook is not used—e.g. *has not been,* *had not been,* *it has been.* In such cases, the hook would not be an advantage and, indeed, would merely cause confusion and loss of legibility.)

(b) *Than*

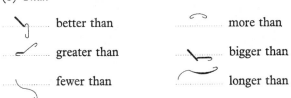

better than    more than

greater than    bigger than

fewer than    longer than

53

### (c) On

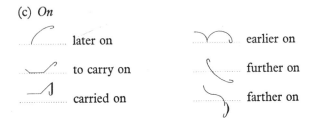

later on      earlier on

to carry on      further on

carried on      farther on

## 2 Addition of there/their

The doubling principle may be applied to phrases such as those shown in 1(a), (b) and (c) in order to add *there/their*:

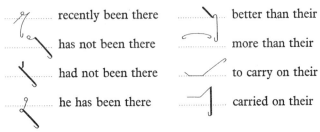

recently been there      better than their

has not been there      more than their

had not been there      to carry on their

he has been there      carried on their

It is obvious that doubled strokes may not be doubled again. Also, where the basic forms are already long, it would be a waste of time (as well as against the rules of lineality) to lengthen such outlines by doubling.

(See also section 12(2), p. 81.)

## 3 Own

*N* hook often represents *own* in phrases. When *own* follows *my*, however, the vocalized stroke is used: ‿‿‿ *my own*. If the hook were used, the resulting outline would read *mine*. The stroke is retained in derivative phrases, such as ‿‿‿ *my own case*; in phrases such as ‿‿ *for his own*, since the hook cannot be written after a circle; and in phrases such as ‿‿‿ *in their own*, following stroke *n*, to ensure absolute clarity.

Examples of the hooked form are:

your own      our own

her own      their own

## 4 Not

*Not* is represented by adding *n* hook and halving the preceding stroke:

⁀ I am not                     ↗ it is certainly not

↗ you will not                 ↗ this will not

⌐ I did not                    ↘ were not

(See also section 11(2b), p. 73.)


## 5 Once/us

*N* hook is used with circle *s* to make the very common phrase ⌐ *at once*. The same principle is seen in ↘ *upon us*.
(See also section 3(5), p. 24.)


## 6 Next

*St* loop is written with right motion to include *n* in order to represent *next*, as in ⌐ *Tuesday next*, ↗ *Wednesday next*.
(See also section 5(3), p. 38.)


## 7 Intersections

Stroke *gay* hooked for *n* is intersected for *beginning*; stroke *v* hooked for *n* is intersected for *convenient/ce*:

⊤ at the beginning             ↗ if it is convenient

⊤ from the beginning          ↗ is it convenient

⊤ from beginning to end        ↗ at your convenience

(See also section 15(2), p. 101.)

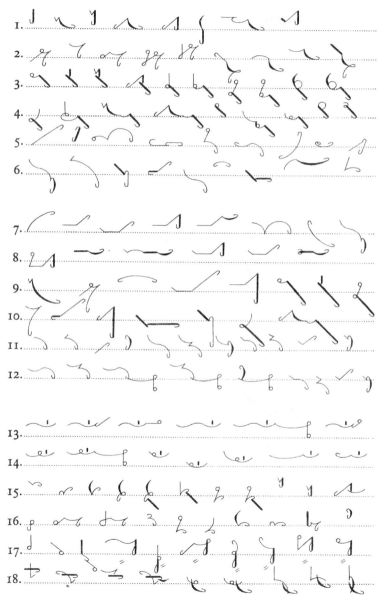

# Practice Material 8

(a)

(b)

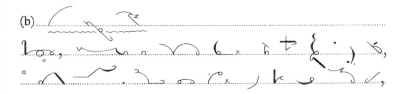

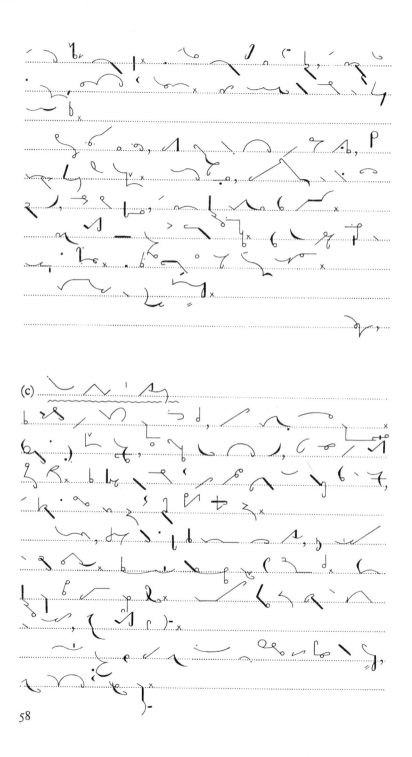

(c)

58

(d)

# Section 9

## F/v Hook

The *f/v* hook may represent the words *have, of* and *off* in phrases. It is also used in phrasing to shorten the outlines for ⟍ *afternoon,* ⟍ *evening,* ⟍ *event* and ⟍ *effect.*

### 1 Simple addition of f/v hook

(a) *Have*

The short form ⟍ is retained in many phrases, such as ⟍ *I have,* ⟍ *as we have,* ⟍ *can only have.* The hook is used in cases where the stroke would not be convenient—particularly, following ╱ and ╭ :

| | | | |
|---|---|---|---|
| ╱ | which have | ╭ | ought to have |
| ╭ | who have | ⟨ | those who have |

(b) *Of*

The hook may, of course, be used only to straight strokes (there being no *f/v* hook to curves). In fact, the most common phrases with *of* (apart from ones where *of* occurs initially) come mainly from outlines ending in *p, t* and *ray*; but there are also some from outlines ending in *b* and *ch/j*:

| | | | |
|---|---|---|---|
| ⟍ | group of | ⌵ | part of |
| ⟍ | capable of | ⟍ | number of |
| ⟩ | plenty of | ⌐ | exchange of |
| ⟩ | state of affairs | ╱ | range of |

(See also section 11(2c), p. 73.)

60

set off        to make off

paid off        better off

wipe off        to take off

## 2 Addition of their/there

The doubling principle may be applied to phrases such as those shown in 1(a), (b) and (c) in order to add *their/there*:

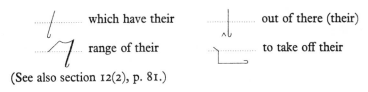

which have their        out of there (their)

range of their        to take off their

(See also section 12(2), p. 81.)

## 3 Afternoon

When the word *afternoon* occurs after an outline ending in *t/d*, it may be represented as a phrase by using *f/v* hook followed by the form ........ :

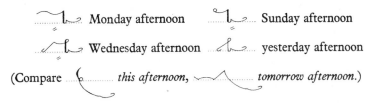

Monday afternoon        Sunday afternoon

Wednesday afternoon        yesterday afternoon

(Compare ........ *this afternoon,* ........ *tomorrow afternoon.*)

## 4 Evening

The remarks concerning *afternoon* apply also to the word *evening*—in this instance, *f/v* hook and the form ........ are used:

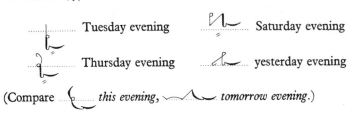

Tuesday evening        Saturday evening

Thursday evening        yesterday evening

(Compare ........ *this evening,* ........ *tomorrow evening.*)

## 5 Event

In a few cases, the hook takes the place of the stroke in phrases containing the word *event*: ......... *at all events,* ......... *such events,* .........
*which events.*

(*Note.* As there is no *f/v* hook to curves, a phrase such as ......... *in
the event* (*of*) must be formed with the stroke.)

## 6 Effect

In phrases, the full form ......... is most often used: ......... *in effect,*
......... *to effect.* Occasionally, it is possible to use the hook, as .........

*into effect.*

# Selected Phrases 9

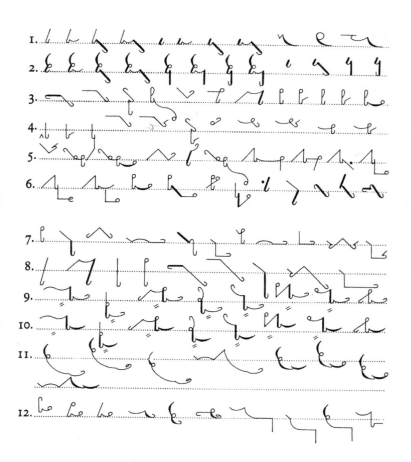

# Practice Material 9

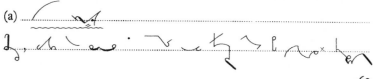

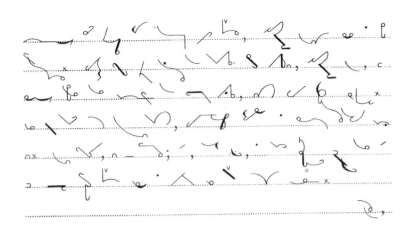

(b)

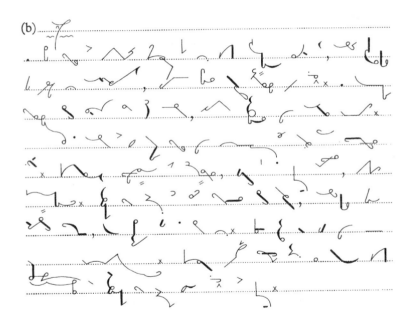

(c)

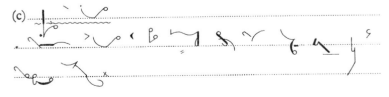

64

(d)

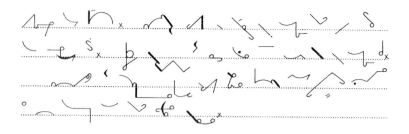

# Section 10

## Shun Hook

The shun hook is used in certain phrases instead of the outlines ⌣ *ocean* and ⌣ *information*. The combination *s-shun*—i.e. the large hook in conjunction with circle *s*—is used in phrases as an abbreviation for the full form ⌣ *association*.

### 1 Ocean

⌣ Arctic Ocean          ⌣ Atlantic Ocean

Compare ⌣ *Indian Ocean,* where the full outline is necessary,

since it is not possible to write *-shun* to another hook.

### 2 Information

⌣ for your information          ⌣ further information

Compare ⌣ *for his information,* ⌣ *any information,* where, if the hook were used, no advantage would be gained and confusion might arise.

### 3 Association

⌣ British Medical Association

⌣ Geographical Association

⌣ your association

⌣ Traders' Association

(See also section 3(6), p. 24.)

When the large hook is written in phrases, it is written to the complete outline; its direction may, therefore, change from that taken when a word stands alone. Compare:

occasion    on such occasions    *but*    on this occasion

section    in these sections    *but*    in some sections

In such circumstances, ease of writing is more important than retaining the original form of the word.

# Selected Phrases 10

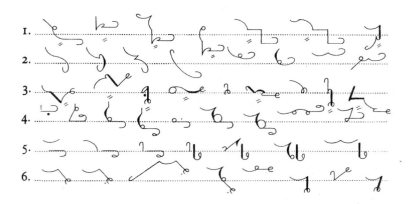

1.
2.
3.
4.
5.
6.

# Practice Material 10

(a)

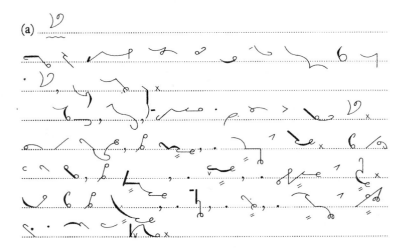

(b)

# Section 11

## Halving Principle

This principle is widely used in phrasing. Some of its uses have already been mentioned briefly (or given as examples) in earlier sections. The principal words, the outlines for which are affected by halving, are dealt with fully below. In each case, only a representative selection of outlines is given, and all suitable opportunities for extending these principles should be explored.

### 1 Simple halving

(a) *It*

In order to represent the word *it* in phrases, the preceding stroke is halved. Further outlines may be joined to such a half-length stroke:

| | | | |
|---|---|---|---|
| ⌣ if it | | ⌐ in which it is | |
| ⌣ if it is | | ⌒ from it | |
| ⌣ if it is not | | ⌒ I think it is necessary | |

A distinction is made in the case of ⌐ *for it* (where the basic outlines join easily, anyway), to avoid any confusion with the half-length form ⌣ *if it*.

(b) *To*

The hooked form *bl* for *able* may be halved for the addition of the word *to*. This principle may also be applied to the *bl* in *unable*. In both cases, additional outlines are easily joined to the half-length forms:

| | |
|---|---|
| ⌐ able to | ⌐ unable to |
| ⌐ able to make | ⌐ unable to make |

......... if we are able to make ...... we are unable to

......... I am able to control

......... I am able to          ......... I am unable to

For the sake of clarity, the phrase *we are not able to* is written ......

and *we are unable to* is written ......... . Disjoining is also used to distinguish other pairs of phrases where similar confusion might otherwise arise (see section 17(2), p. 129).

## 2 Hooks

(a) *R*

As has already been mentioned, the hooked form *pr* is halved to represent the word *part* in phrases:

......... for my part          ......... greater part (of)

......... all parts            ......... larger part (of)

......... all parts of the world   ......... other parts

(See also section 6(1d), p. 42.)

In exactly the same way, the hooked form ......... may be halved to represent *board* in phrases:

......... board of directors   ......... Electricity Board

......... board and lodging    ......... your board

(*Note.* As is usual, when the word *board* stands alone, the full outline is necessary: ......... . The full form is also used where it gives a better outline or where the half-length stroke does not join easily: .........
*British Railways Board.*)

(b) *N*

Phrases containing the word *not* are formed by adding *n* hook and halving the preceding stroke:

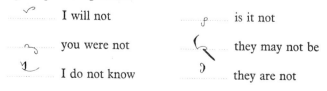

......... I will not           ......... is it not

......... you were not         ......... they may not be

......... I do not know        ......... they are not

(*Note.* In a few cases, halving is not applied—e.g. ⌣ *have not,*

⌣ *are not,* ⌣ *was not,* ⌣ *we are not*—as better outlines, which are more quickly identified in transcription, are achieved by retaining the full stroke.)

Colloquial forms such as *don't* are distinguished by vocalization and sometimes involve a change of outline. Compare the following:

| | | | |
|---|---|---|---|
| do not | don't | did not | didn't |
| shall not | shan't | will not | won't |
| are not | aren't | cannot | can't |
| have not | haven't | is not | isn't |
| was not | wasn't | were not | weren't |
| would not | wouldn't | should not | shouldn't |

(See also section 8(4), p. 55, and section 17(4), p. 131.)


## (c) *F/v*

Examples are to be found in section 9 of the small final hook representing *of* following a half-length stroke, as:

| | |
|---|---|
| sort of | part of |
| in spite of | present state of |
| instead of | present state of affairs |

The *f/v* hook is not used, however, when *part* is represented by the half-length stroke ⌐. In this way, it is possible to make a clear distinction between *part of* and *number of*. For example, compare

⌐ *great part (of)* and ⌐ *great number of;* ⌐ *large part (of) the* and ⌐ *large number of the.*

(See also section 9(1b), p. 60.)

### 3 Change of form

#### (a) *Out*

The preceding stroke is halved and the diphthong added to represent the word *out*, as follows:

set out     brought out

carried out     to set out

#### (b) *State*

Instead of the full form with *st* loop, the word (or syllable) *state* may be represented by the half-length form　ᴾ　:

to state     in their statement

this state     this statement

recent statement     several statements

#### (c) *Time*

The word *time* in phrases is usually represented by halving the preceding stroke and adding *m*:

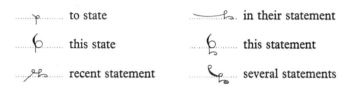

at some time     from time to time

at the same time     at all times

for some time past     lunch time

at one time     spare time

When *time* follows an outline that is already halved, it is necessary simply to add stroke *m*, as ⌒ *short time.*

The basic rule that strokes of unequal length may not be joined unless there is an angle between them applies to phrases as well as to outlines for individual words. It is, therefore, not possible to use the

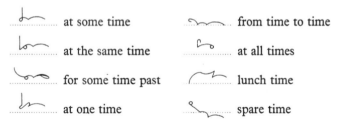

halving principle when *time* follows stroke *n*: ⌒ *no time,*　⌐　*at any time.* In the phrase *at no time* ⌐ it is necessary to insert the vowel in *no* in order to distinguish it from *at any time.*

**(d)** *Word/would*

The half-length stroke ⟋ is used in phrases instead of (i) ⟍ and (ii) ⟋ when the short forms do not join easily:

(i)      in those words      in other words

           in his own words      few words

           common words      to say a few words

(ii)      I would      this would

           we would be      if it would be

           they would not be      that would

(*Note.* Compare    *in the words*,    *words a minute*;    *it would be*,    *he would not*—where no benefit would be gained by using   ⟋ .)

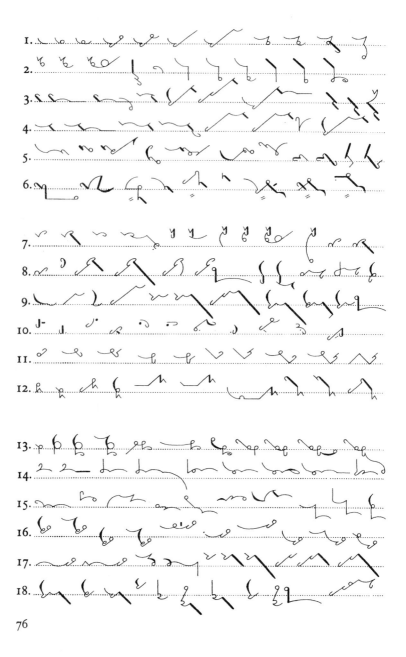

# Practice Material 11

(a) (i)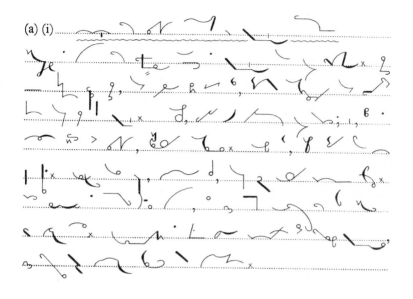

(ii)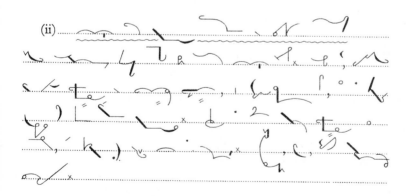

(iii)

(b)

(c)

# Section 12

## *Doubling Principle*

This principle is used in phrasing mainly to represent the words *their/there* and *other*. Doubling is also used in certain phrases with *therefore* and *order*, a change of form being involved. These uses are fully explained below.

There is a good deal of scope for individual writers to adapt the doubling principle to suit their own particular needs. It is perhaps worth repeating that, in order to be effective, any extension of the principles set out in this section (or any extension of other principles in other sections) must conform to the basic rules of facility, lineality and legibility.

### 1 Simple Doubling

(a) *Their/there*

Strokes may be doubled for the addition of *their/there*. As with doubling in word outlines, it is important that the double length of the stroke be clearly shown. To ensure absolute clarity, it may be wise to exaggerate the length slightly, rather than to write a precisely doubled stroke. Further outlines will join easily to the double-length forms.

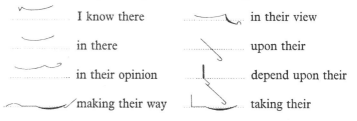

I know there    in their view

in there    upon their

in their opinion    depend upon their

making their way    taking their

Circle *s* may be added to such a stroke; it is read last after the double-length stroke to which it is written:

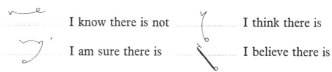

I know there is not    I think there is

I am sure there is    I believe there is

(b) *Other*

Strokes may also be doubled for the addition of *other*. For practical purposes, this applies almost entirely to strokes *m* and *n*. Again, further outlines may be joined to the double-length strokes so formed.

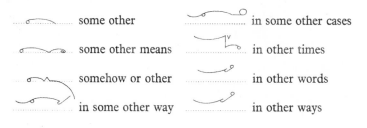

| | |
|---|---|
| some other | in some other cases |
| some other means | in other times |
| somehow or other | in other words |
| in some other way | in other ways |

The outlines _____ *any other* and _____ *no other* are not doubled, *r* hook being omitted to make the phrase in each case. The doubled stroke must be used in _____ *another* and could easily clash in context with *any other*. A second-position doubled *n* (which represents many words) could well be misread or lead to loss of time in transcription if it were also used to represent the phrase *no other*.

(*Note.* In addition, doubling may be used to represent the word *dear*, though one meets such phrases less often nowadays. In most cases the *dear* follows *my*, as _____ *my dear friend*, _____ *my dear Miss Brown*.)

## 2 Hooks

As has been seen already in sections 8 and 9, doubling may be applied to strokes hooked for *n* or *f/v*:

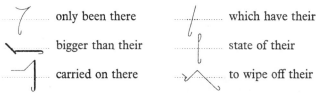

| | |
|---|---|
| only been there | which have their |
| bigger than their | state of their |
| carried on there | to wipe off their |

It is obviously necessary to make a distinction between *for there is* (*has*) and *if there is* (*has*). That is achieved by using simple joining for the former— _____ *for there is* (*has*)—and applying the normal doubling to the latter— _____ *if there is* (*has*).

81

## 3 Change of form

### (a) *Therefore*

In a few cases, doubling is used with *fr* to represent *therefore*. That avoids disjoining, which would otherwise be necessary:

I shall therefore       I was therefore

The principle is applied only where there is some advantage to be gained from its use. Notice ⁀ *I have therefore* and ⁀ *I think therefore*, where the ordinary form joins without difficulty.

### (b) *Order*

As mentioned in section 6, doubling is used with *r* hook when *order* follows *in*:

in order       in order that you may

in order that we know       in order that he will

The phrase *in order to* cannot safely be formed just by adding the short form ( ⁀ ) to the double-length stroke for *in order*. It is therefore written as follows: ⁀ *in order to*. Further outlines may be added to the hooked form.
(See also section 6(2c), p. 43.)

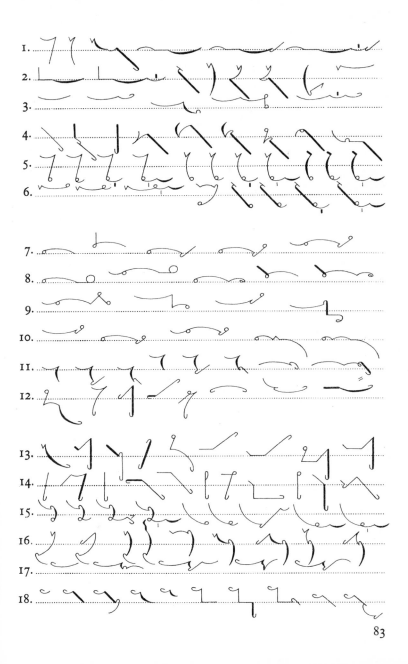

# Practice Material 12

(a)

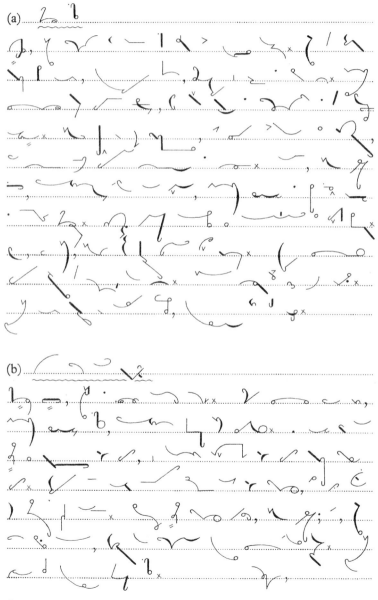

(b)

(c)

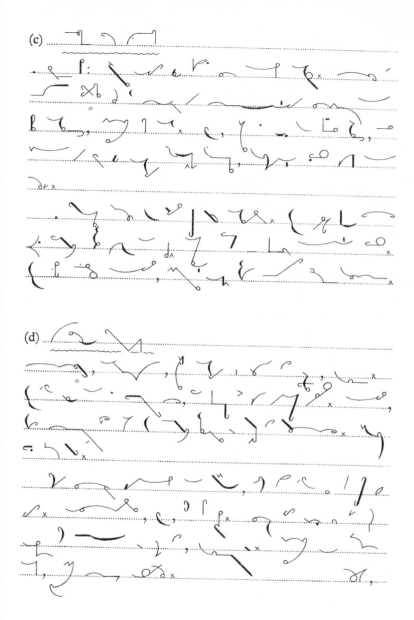

(d)

# Section 13

## *Consonants R, L, W, H*

The basic rules of the Pitman system provide for each of these consonants to be written in more than one way. It is sometimes possible, by using a different form of the consonant from that required in the individual outlines for certain words, to achieve a better outline in a phrase. In some cases, the scope of such words in phrasing is also extended.

### 1 Consonant R

Words in which the form of *r* is changed when they occur in phrases are—*were* ( ), *war* ( ), *wire* ( ), *sir* ( ), *per* ( ), *appear* ( ), *door* ( ):

| | | | |
|---|---|---|---|
| they were | | telephone wire |
| we were | | Sir James |
| if it were | | yes, sir |
| before the war | | per annum |
| during the war | | per cent |
| after the war | | per head |
| live wire | | it would appear |
| several wires | | out of doors |

As can be seen, in phrases containing the outline for *war*, a better joining is sometimes obtained by including tick *the*, whilst in other cases it is better omitted.

(See also section 6(1b), p. 41.)

## 2 Consonant L

In order to keep the outlines for certain phrases within the rules for upward and downward *l*, the stroke is sometimes written to the phrase as a whole. This may involve changing the direction that the stroke would take if it were written in an individual outline:

(a) *Preceding or following circle s*

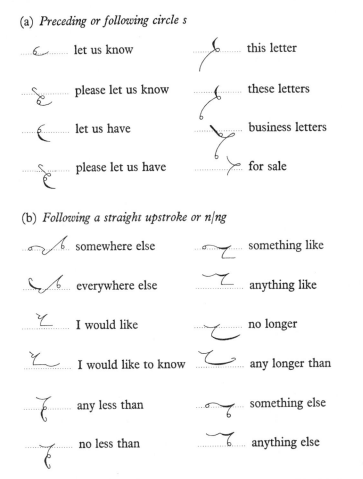

let us know

please let us know

let us have

please let us have

this letter

these letters

business letters

for sale

(b) *Following a straight upstroke or n/ng*

somewhere else

everywhere else

I would like

I would like to know

any less than

no less than

something like

anything like

no longer

any longer than

something else

anything else

(*Note.* I *should* like could also be rendered as a phrase with the downward *l*—as in I *would* like, but omitting the   —  . There should be no confusion with    I *like*, as that, of course, is written with the contracted diphthong before *upward l*.)

87

## 3 Consonant W

### (a) Omission

The initial semi-circle or hook is often omitted in phrases containing the words *week, were, will, well*:

this week                     so well

next week                   very well

last week                    very well indeed

you will                      who were

I will not                    you were

that he will                  you were not

In _____ *this will*, the *l* goes down because it follows the motion of the circle. In the phrase _____ *we will*, the abbreviated form is not used.
(See also section 16(1f), p. 117.)

### (b) Stroke w

The stroke is used instead of the semi-circle if a better joining results:

in the world                  all over the world

throughout the world          in this world

Some similar examples have already been given in the paragraph on *Consonant R* at the beginning of this Section: e.g. _____ *telephone wires*, _____ *during the war*, _____ *they were*; but in those cases consonants *w* and *r* have both changed their form.

### (c) Was

Stroke *way* with circle *s* is sometimes better than the short form _____ , as in these phrases:

that was                      this was

that was not                  this was not

Note the difference between ⌇ *that was not* and ⌇ *this was not* as compared with ⌇ *that wasn't* and ⌇ *this wasn't*, where vocalization is used to show the distinction.

## (d) *Weeks*

Although this word is often written as shown in paragraph 3(a) on page 88—by omitting the initial semi-circle—in a few cases stroke *w* gives a better joining than stroke *k*:

⌇ several weeks ⌇ past few weeks

## (e) *As-w*

*Sw* circle is used to represent an initial sound of *w* preceded by *as*:

⌇ as well as ⌇ as will be seen

⌇ as we can ⌇ as well as possible

(See also section 4(1b), p. 31.)

## 4 Consonant H

*H* is omitted in some phrases. For instance, the outline for *house* ( ⌇ ) changes its form completely and is represented by stroke *s*; *hope* ( ⌇ ) drops the initial stroke consonant and is represented by stroke *p*; *home* ( ⌇ ) loses its tick *h* and is represented by stroke *m*:

⌇ to the house ⌇ I hope there is

⌇ in the House of Commons ⌇ at home

⌇ I hope that you will ⌇ at home and overseas

It is very important to distinguish between *him/himself* and *me/myself* in phrases, as context is of little or no help in transcription. Phrases with *him/himself* are vocalized, while *me/myself* phrases are not:

⌇ of him ⌇ of me

⌇ from him ⌇ from me

⌇ for himself ⌇ for myself

⌇ by himself ⌇ by myself

89

Medial tick *h* is written only in phrases:

....... by whom                      ....... in here

....... for whom                     ....... for her

....... to here (hear)               ....... of her own

Notice particularly ....... *over here* but ....... *overhear.*

# Selected Phrases 13

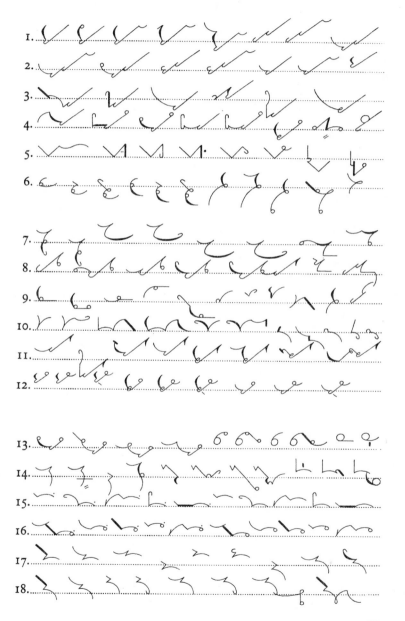

# Practice Material 13

(a)

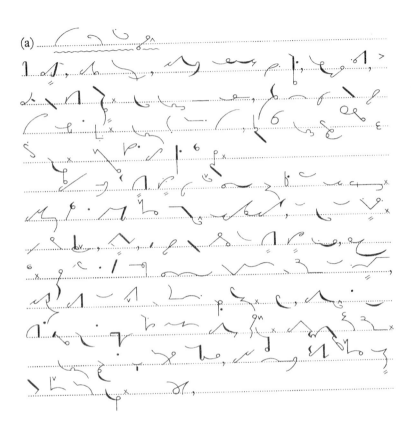

(b)

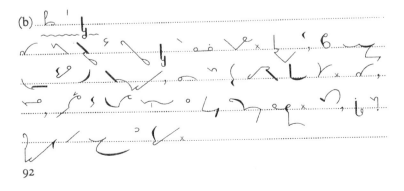

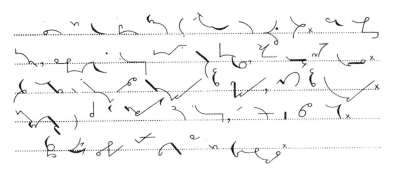

(c)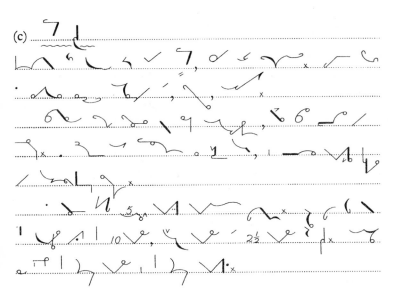

(d)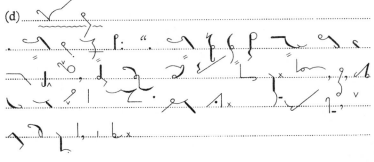

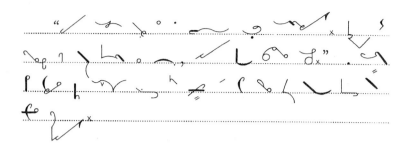

# Section 14

## *Prefixes and Suffixes*

The prefixes *con-/com-* and certain suffixes can be usefully adapted to phrasing. Where a suffix takes the form of a complete word (such as *-logical* or *-ship*), the sign for the suffix may be used in phrases to represent that word.

### 1 Prefixes

(a) *Proximity for con-/com-*

In a word, *con-/com-* may occur medially and be indicated by writing the preceding and following parts of the outline close to each other to show the position of the omitted syllable (such as ⟋ *recommend*). In phrases, too, the dot may be left out and the prefix indicated by proximity:

...... in control      ...... in committee

...... unable to consider      ...... unfair competition

...... it is continuous      ...... it has been completed

...... in connection (with)      ...... many commitments

The phrase ...... *income tax* is formed by extending the same principle.

(b) *Non-use of proximity*

In all the phrases shown above, the closing up saves time and is quite clear. However, compare the following:

...... all conditions      ...... and conditions

...... on committees      ...... on the committee

95

....⌐.... the contract          ...⌐.... in the contract

....'S.... a complaint          ...'S.... minor complaint

It is obvious that it would not be possible to achieve sufficient clarity if proximity were used with a single downward dash short form or the dots for *a* and *the*. In such circumstances, the outlines must be separated and the *con-/com-* dot written.

### (c) *Omission*

In a few phrases that occur very frequently, the prefix (either in the form of a dot or indicated by proximity) is omitted altogether:

....⌐.... it is considered          ...⌐.... in conclusion

....⌐.... it is to be considered          ...⌐.... come to the conclusion

Any writer wishing to extend this principle should take particular care to test a proposed phrase and ensure its legibility before adopting it for general use.

(See also section 16(2), p. 119.)

### 2 Suffixes

The following examples show how the single strokes representing suffixes may be extended to represent complete words in phrases. This is a sophisticated principle and, as such, is of more value to writers of some experience. Those at a fairly elementary level would do well to consolidate basic rules of phrasing and postpone the learning and practice of such principles as those explained below until they reach a more advanced stage.

#### (a) *Ability*

....\.... your ability          ....\.... best of your ability

....\.... our ability          ....\.... best of our ability

#### (b) *Reality*

....⌐.... in reality          ....⌐.... there is no reality

....⌐.... no reality          ....⌐.... to face reality

(c) *Logical*

_____ it would be logical _____ it is not logical

_____ you are not logical _____ if we are logical

(d) *Mentality*

_____ of low mentality _____ of this mentality

_____ your mentality _____ poor mentality

(e) *Ship(ment)*

_____ this ship _____ these ships

_____ new ship _____ for shipment

_____ several ships _____ some shipments

(f) *Fullness*

_____ in the fullness of time

(g) *Yard*

_____ several yards _____ dozen yards

The half-length *yay* for *yard* should not be used when the short form _____ joins easily—e.g. _____ *two yards*.

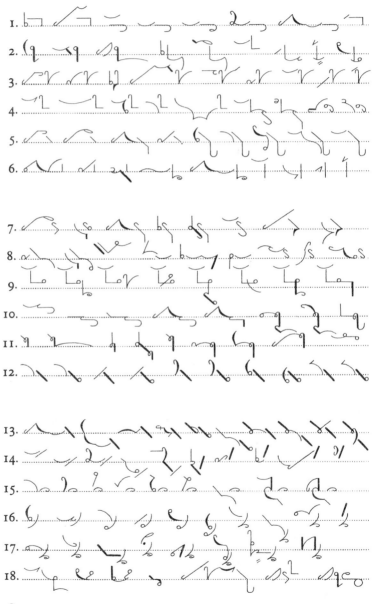

# Practice Material 14

(a)

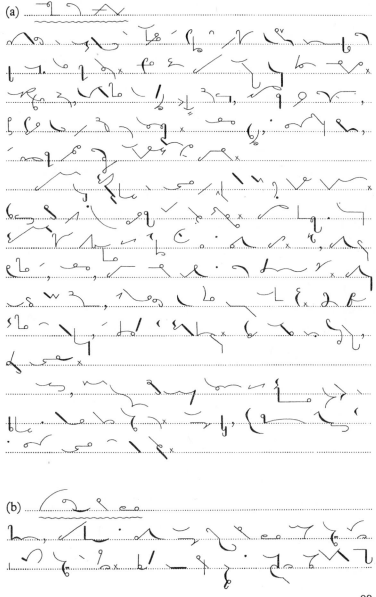

(b)

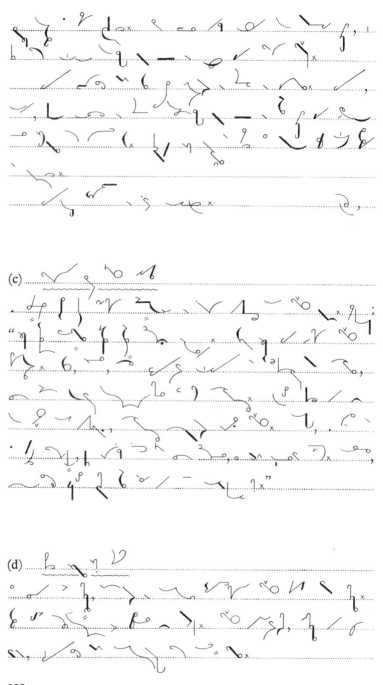

(c)

(d)

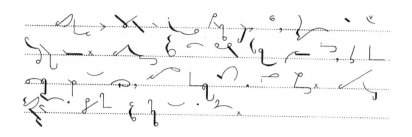

# Section 15

## *Intersections*

Single strokes representing whole words may be intersected through other outlines in order to make phrases. There are times when it is not possible actually to intersect—usually when the stroke to be intersected and the intersection itself are written in the same direction (such as *p* and *b*, *k* and *g*). The intersection is then written before or after, but parallel with, the other stroke involved: ⟋⟍ *Labour Party,* ⟋ *new capital,* ⟋ *Chancery Judge,* ═══ *Captain Cook.*

It is always helpful from the writer's point of view to write the words in the order in which they are spoken, so that the continuity of the writing may be maintained. By placing the intersection accordingly (e.g. ┼ *captain of the team,* ∟ *team captain*), it is possible to indicate whether the intersection should be read first or last. In the case of single-stroke outlines, such a distinction is not possible (e.g. ⟍ *your enquiry*), though it is still important to write the words in the same order as that in which they are spoken. Provided the words are read in context and common sense is applied, no difficulty should be experienced because of the lack of precise indication of word order.

Intersections do not have positions of their own. The position of an intersected stroke is automatically adjusted according to its position in the outline through which it is struck. That can be seen in the following examples: ⟋⟍ *party manifesto,* ⟋⟍ *party games,* ∟ *dinner party.*

Intersections may be classified under three headings: (1) standard, (2) advanced, (3) special.

# I STANDARD INTERSECTIONS

These should be useful to (and used by) all practising shorthand writers:

| | | | |
|---|---|---|---|
| p/party | | party leader | | birthday party |
| pr/professor | | Professor Jones | | Music Professor |
| spr/ superintendent | | superintendent of parks | | police superintendent |
| b/bank | | bank clerk | | Lloyds Bank |
| | | Bank of England | | Barclays Bank |
| -bankment | | river embankment | | Thames Embankment |
| bill | | bill of sale | | Private Member's Bill |
| t/attention | | some attention | | immediate attention |
| | | for your attention | | draw your attention to the fact |
| d/department | | Department of Commerce | | in several departments |
| | | department stores | | Housing Department |
| ch/charge-d | | handling charge | | higher charges |
| | | free of charge | | you will be charged |
| Chancery | | Chancery Appeal | | Chancery Judge |
| j/journal | | journal entries | | professional journal |
| | | house journal | | trade journal |
| k/company | | company auditors | | ballet company |
| capital | | capital city | | issued capital |
| | | capital letters | | new capital |
| council | | council chamber | | County Council |
| captain | | captain of the ship | | group captain |

103

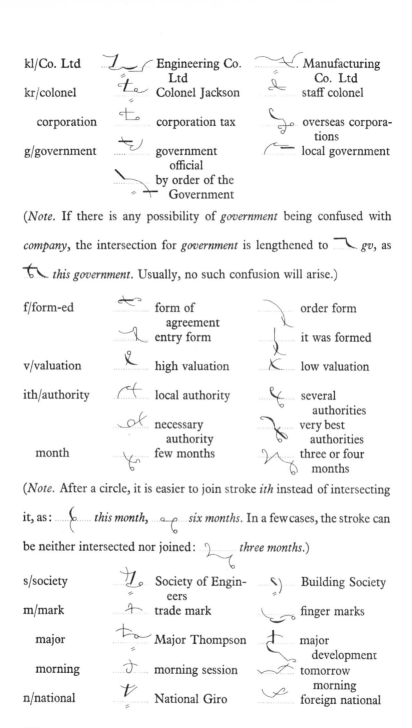

kl/Co. Ltd    Engineering Co. Ltd    Manufacturing Co. Ltd

kr/colonel    Colonel Jackson    staff colonel

corporation    corporation tax    overseas corporations

g/government    government official    local government

by order of the Government

(*Note.* If there is any possibility of *government* being confused with *company*, the intersection for *government* is lengthened to ⌐ *gv*, as ⌐ *this government*. Usually, no such confusion will arise.)

f/form-ed    form of agreement    order form

entry form    it was formed

v/valuation    high valuation    low valuation

ith/authority    local authority    several authorities

necessary authority    very best authorities

month    few months    three or four months

(*Note.* After a circle, it is easier to join stroke *ith* instead of intersecting it, as: *this month*, *six months*. In a few cases, the stroke can be neither intersected nor joined: *three months*.)

s/society    Society of Engineers    Building Society

m/mark    trade mark    finger marks

major    Major Thompson    major development

morning    morning session    tomorrow morning

n/national    National Giro    foreign national

104

| | | |
|---|---|---|
| enquire-d-y | will you enquire | letter of enquiry |
| inquire-d-y | for your inquiry | police inquiries |
| l/liberal | Liberal Party | liberal measures |
| limited | limited company | Selfridges Ltd |
| ar/arrange-d-ment | you can arrange | this arrangement |
| ray/railway | it has been arranged | please make arrangements |
| | railway station | miniature railway |
| | British Railways Board | private railways |
| require-d-ment | do you require | estimated requirement |
| | when it is required | substantial requirements |
| s-ray/conservative | Conservative Party | conservative estimates |

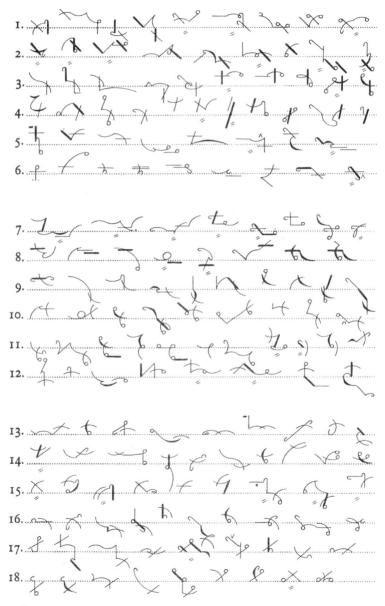

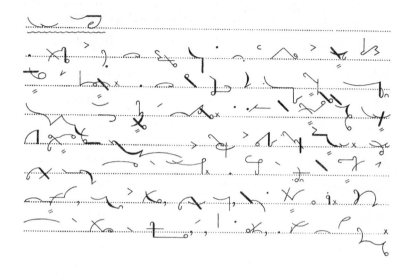

# 2 ADVANCED INTERSECTIONS

The intersections that follow are more suitable for writers of some experience. (*Note.* Writers at a less advanced level should make sure that all the standard intersections can be written fluently and without hesitation before proceeding further. To try to learn too many intersections at once may result in none being learned thoroughly.)

| p/policy | ⟍⟍ | policy of the Board | ⟍ | life policies |

p/policy — policy of the Board — life policies

b/bishop — Bishop of Coventry — Roman Catholic Bishop

f/forth — hold forth — bring forth

(*Note.* ⟨ *set forth*—see section 6(2f), p. 43.)

s/scientific — scientific research — scientific work

pl/application — to make application — form of application

pn/punishment — judicial punishment — severe punishment

bs/business — business dealings — new business

(*Note.* When ⟍ *bs* precedes strokes such as *m*, *l* and *ray*, it is sometimes joined, as: ⟍ *business man,* ⟍ *business life,* ⟍ *business relations.*)

gn/beginning — at the beginning — from the beginning to the end

vn/convenient-ence — is it convenient — at your convenience

sh-s/assurance — life assurance — endowment assurance

sm/similar — similar letters — similar results

ns/insurance — comprehensive insurance — marine insurance

n-shun/com-munication — any (in) com-munication — further com-munication

# Selected Phrases 15B

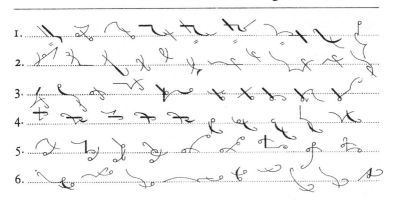

1.
2.
3.
4.
5.
6.

# Practice Material 15B

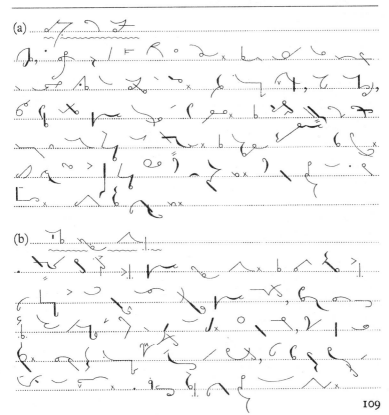

(a)

(b)

# 3 SPECIAL INTERSECTIONS

Such intersections may be devised by an experienced practising writer in a specialized field of work. For instance, a writer whose work contains many references to insurance will probably use the intersections given in the advanced section for *policy* ⟨ ⟩, *insurance* ⟨ ⟩ and *assurance* ⟨ ⟩. Equally, with material covering other topics, the *p* could be intersected to make the phrase ⟨ ⟩ *post code*; the *ns* to make the phrase ⟨ ⟩ *interstellar research*; the *sh-s* to make the phrase ⟨ ⟩ *Austrian schillings*.

The intersection of *b* for *bishop* would be particularly useful to someone using theological vocabulary or to the reporter of a synod. Someone working in a laboratory might put it to better use to represent *bacteriological* ⟨ ⟩, as in ⟨ ⟩ *bacteriological culture*; or someone reporting meteorological vocabulary could write ⟨ ⟩ for *barometric pressure*.

One of the most useful aspects of intersections is that they are adaptable to changes in the language. In the days before atomic power and the hydrogen bomb, no one would have required intersections for the phrases ⟨ ⟩ *atomic power station* and ⟨ ⟩ *hydrogen bomb*. Until the discovery of uranium, no special sign was needed for that word; now ⟨ ⟩ *uranium ore* is a perfectly good use for an intersected *yay*. If *uranium* is met with seldom but *Europe* and *European* occur very frequently, then *yay* and *yay-n* might be adapted to represent those words: ⟨ ⟩ *Northern Europe*, ⟨ ⟩ *European Parliament*.

This very adaptability can lead to difficulties if shorthand writers do not exercise care and thought *before* adopting an intersection into their practical vocabularies. For example, in the scientific field, it might be tempting to intersect *t* both for *atomic* and for *titanium*. A little thought beforehand would perhaps result in *t* ⟨ ⟩ being intersected for *atomic*, while *titanium* could be distinguished by intersecting *t-n* ⟨ ⟩. Again, *ray* might be intersected for *radio* or *radar*; to intersect for both might well lead to inaccuracy in transcription.

It would be difficult to find a subject where the vocabulary would not lend itself to some form of intersection. The only "rule" that need be observed (apart from the invariable ones of facility, lineality and legibility) is that of common sense. The principles set out here may be usefully applied to any topic, provided clashes are anticipated and that intersections are devised only for words occurring frequently in combination with others. (See also section 19.)

The following list shows a number of miscellaneous phrases that incorporate intersections—though, again, in some cases (such as *ray* for *already*) it would be possible to extend them to similar combinations:

| | | | |
|---|---|---|---|
| | in pursuance | | for this purpose |
| | speaking from memory | | if you will kindly |
| | value added tax | | atomic power station |
| | no alternative | | limited liability company |
| | in the House of Commons | | vote of thanks |
| | North and South America | | from time im- memorial |
| | United Nations | | at right angles |
| | best of my recollection | | rank and file |
| | we have already | | Royal Commission |

# Selected Phrases 15C

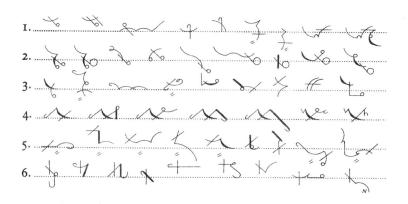

# Practice Material 15C

# PART THREE

## Advanced Principles

The principles set out in the following sections are of more value to experienced writers and to those who are attempting fairly high speeds. It is no reflection on the skill of someone who is writing at, say, 80 wpm to be cautioned against trying to learn too much at once. A half-learned rule can be a very real danger to the shorthand writer—and it is a danger that is often not recognized until after the damage has been done.

It is pointless to attempt to learn too many principles at one time, or before the earlier principles have been mastered and are able to be applied without thought. The probable result of such "cramming" is that little or no benefit will be derived, and the rate of writing may drop (because of mental confusion) rather than increase.

Provided the principles explained in previous sections have been sufficiently drilled and practised, it should be possible for the more advanced devices in this Part to be tackled without difficulty.

# Section 16

## *Principle of Omission*

Examples of omission have already been seen in earlier sections. Here the subject is dealt with more fully. Omission is one of the most rewarding of all principles of phrasing. By leaving out a consonant, a syllable, or a whole word (in some cases, more than one word), phrases may be created that are not only very quick to write but also easy to read back. For instance, the omission of the *t* following *s* in ⌇ *bes(t) way* or ⌒ *mos(t) important* should cause no difficulty in transcription, and it does offer a very real saving of time. In the same way, when a consonant is repeated, as in ⌇ *prime (m)inister* or ⌒ *animal (l)ife*, it is often quite safe to use one written consonant to represent the two spoken ones.

Even omitted syllables and words are generally ones that would be apparent just from looking at the longhand. In "We send these samples for your sideration", it does not require a genius to realize that the syllable *con-* has been omitted. It is a matter of simple common sense, in studying the sentence "The proposal that we should embark on a policy of capital expenditure at such a time is quite out question", to see that the words *of the* must be inserted between *out* and *question*. This "natural" omission is reflected in the shorthand outlines: ⌇ *for your consideration* and ⌇ *out of the question.*

There is in this principle scope for extreme abbreviation of quite long sentences. It would not, however, be very sensible to use a short-cut for examination purposes, or in any practical situation, without trying it out first. If in testing a proposed short-cut in the class-room or in practice dictation at home an outline is mistranscribed, nothing very serious is likely to result—except perhaps the abandonment of that particular short-cut. If it were used by a secretary in an office, damage might be done to her reputation for efficiency. For the Hansard reporter or an official note-taker in court, such a humiliation would be emphasized by the inaccuracy being to some extent public.

It must also be remembered that what is reasonable in one set of circumstances is not necessarily reasonable in another. For instance, extreme application of the principle of omission (or any other principle) is wise only if the phrase to which it is applied is well known and written frequently. This is particularly true of proper names. If for some reason a writer has to write a long name, with perhaps difficult outlines, it is sensible to use omission to produce a clear and fast outline. This might apply to a secretary who has to record regular reports about a particular firm or to a note-taker reporting a court case in which the name features prominently. This use of the principles of phrasing is highly specialized. Unless care and thought have been given to the outline to be used, difficulties could easily arise in transcription. For that reason, it would be a most unwise procedure for an examination candidate.

The principles illustrated are capable of considerable extension, either generally or to specific requirements.

Although the following outlines are listed under headings of the omitted consonant, syllable or word, **it will be noticed that in some cases other omissions are made in the same outline, and some changes of form are also involved.**

## 1 OMISSION OF A CONSONANT

(a) *T(d) following s*

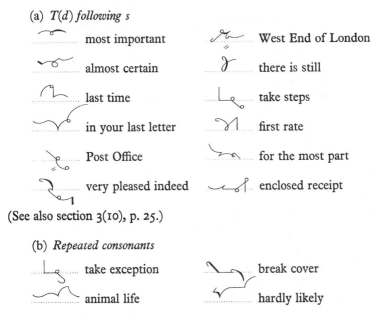

|  |  |
|---|---|
| most important | West End of London |
| almost certain | there is still |
| last time | take steps |
| in your last letter | first rate |
| Post Office | for the most part |
| very pleased indeed | enclosed receipt |

(See also section 3(10), p. 25.)

(b) *Repeated consonants*

|  |  |
|---|---|
| take exception | break cover |
| animal life | hardly likely |

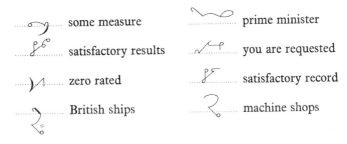

some measure

satisfactory results

zero rated

British ships

prime minister

you are requested

satisfactory record

machine shops

(*Note.* In the examples _____ *poor results* and _____ *political life*, it will be seen that the principle may be applied even though the first consonant is not written in the same way as the second—unrepresented —one.)

(c) *R* (*hook*)

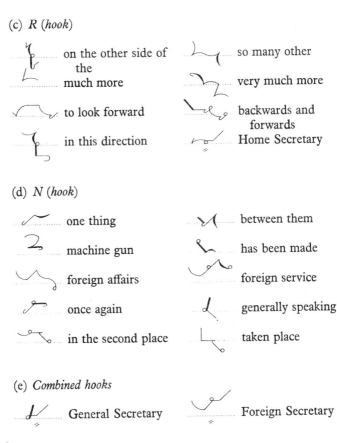

on the other side of the

much more

to look forward

in this direction

so many other

very much more

backwards and forwards

Home Secretary

(d) *N* (*hook*)

one thing

machine gun

foreign affairs

once again

in the second place

between them

has been made

foreign service

generally speaking

taken place

(e) *Combined hooks*

General Secretary

Foreign Secretary

116

## (f) *Miscellaneous*

in fact

worth while

long life

it will be

I hope there is

at home

this week

very well

# Selected Phrases 16A

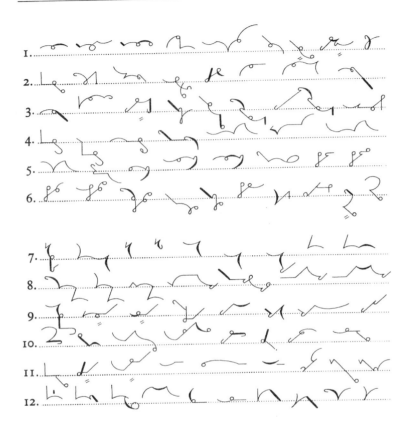

# Practice Material 16A

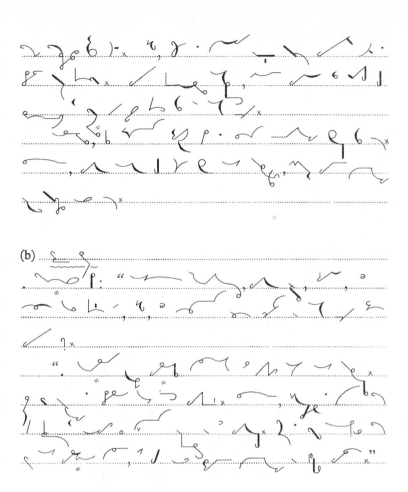

(b)

## 2 OMISSION OF A SYLLABLE

| | | | |
|---|---|---|---|
| **con-** | we have concluded | | for your consideration |
| | satisfactory conclusion | | to consider |
| | we are concerned | | in consequence (of) |
| **ex-** | great expense | | personal experience |
| | heavy expenses | | recent experiences |
| **fa-** | very favourable | | more favourable |
| **-hand** | shorthand writer | | shorthand writing |
| **here-** | enclose herewith | | to send herewith |
| **-ible** | if possible | | as soon as possible |
| | if it is not possible | | as early as possible |
| **in-** | your instructions | | if you will instruct |
| | I am instructed | | musical instrument |
| **-ingdom** | Kingdom of the Netherlands | | United Kingdom |
| **-ish** | British Museum | | British Isles |
| | British manufacture | | British people |
| **-ly** | extremely sorry | | distinctly understood |
| **ma-** | in this manner | | in the same manner |
| **-ment** | Act of Parliament | | Member of Parliament |
| **-nical** | technical progress | | Technical College |
| | technical terms | | technical difficulty |

| | | |
|---|---|---|
| **ob-** | we have no objection | there is no objection |
| **pre-** | high pressure | low pressure |
| | extreme pressure | water pressure |
| **re-** | in reply | in reply to your letter |
| | in regard (to) | we shall be glad to receive |
| | we have received | as regards |
| **-sty** | Her Majesty | His Majesty |
| | Her Majesty the Queen | His Majesty the King |
| **-ted** | I am requested to inform you | you are requested to call |

(*Note*. The outline for *also*—⌒⌒—is sometimes abbreviated in phrases to ⌒, as you may also, it is also.)

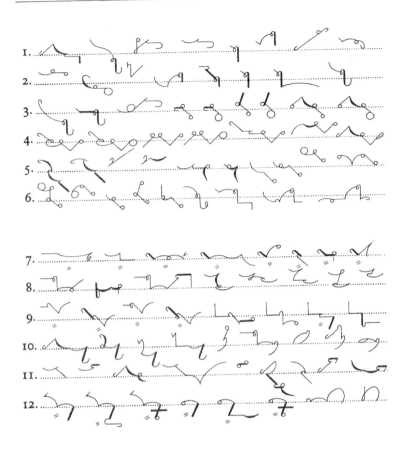

## Practice Material *16B*

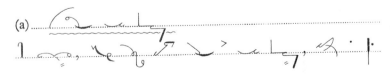

(b)

## 3 OMISSION OF WORDS

| | | | |
|---|---|---|---|
| **a/an** | ⌐ for a time | ⌐ half a million | |
| | ⌐ at a loss | ⌐ as a rule | |
| **and** | ⌐ now and then | ⌐ first and foremost | |
| | ⌐ here and there | ⌐ over and above | |
| | ⌐ larger and larger | ⌐ more and more | |
| **(syllable) and** | ⌐ bigger and bigger | ⌐ tighter and tighter | |
| | ⌐ longer and longer | ⌐ thinner and thinner | |
| | ⌐ higher and higher | ⌐ rougher and rougher | |

(*Note.* In phrases such as ⌐ *faster and faster* and ⌐ *nearer and nearer*, the principle is modified slightly, as there is no need to separate the forms.)

| | | | |
|---|---|---|---|
| **by** | ⌐ side by side | ⌐ year by year | |
| **come (to the)** | ⌐ I have come to the conclusion | ⌐ we have come to the conclusion | |
| **have** | ⌐ there have been | ⌐ seems to have been | |
| | ⌐ would have been | ⌐ it must have been | |
| **in** | ⌐ bear in mind | ⌐ stock in trade | |
| | ⌐ borne in mind | ⌐ cash in hand | |
| **into** | ⌐ to take into consideration | ⌐ to take into account | |
| **nor** | ⌐ neither more nor less | ⌐ neither this nor that | |
| **of** | ⌐ difference of opinion | ⌐ some of them | |
| | ⌐ expression of opinion | ⌐ standard of living | |
| | ⌐ point of view | ⌐ years of age | |
| | ⌐ in the form (of) | ⌐ City of London | |

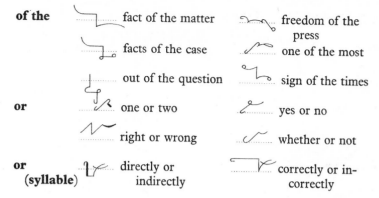

**of the**    fact of the matter    freedom of the press

facts of the case    one of the most

out of the question    sign of the times

**or**    one or two    yes or no

right or wrong    whether or not

**or (syllable)**    directly or indirectly    correctly or incorrectly

(*Note.* Special care must be taken in extending this particular principle to ensure that confusion does not arise. For example, ⟍ could be reasonably transcribed as either *competent enquiry* or *competent or incompetent*. Such combinations are obviously potentially dangerous.)

**the**    what is the matter    in the first instance

in the circumstances    in the event (of)

on the subject    in the hands (of)

in the past    for the sake (of)

**to**    I am sorry to say    that is to say

needless to say    in reply to the

in addition to the    having regard to

with regard to the    ought to have been

**to the**    come to the conclusion    up to the present

came to the conclusion    up to the present time

your attention to the matter    call attention to the matter

**with**    in connection with    in connection with the

**you**    will you please    if you please

# Selected Phrases 16C

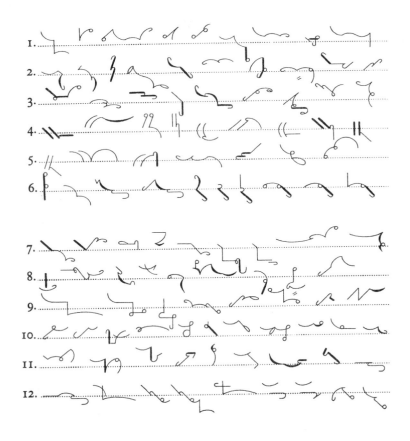

# Practice Material 16C

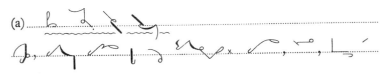

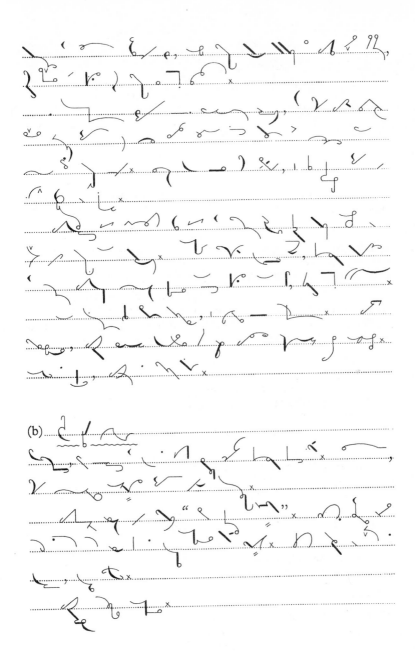

# Section 17

## *Making Distinctions*

In single outlines it is sometimes necessary to distinguish between those that have an almost identical structure. That may be achieved by vocalization (compare  *amusing* and  *amazing*;  *specialist* and  *specialized*) or by changing the form of one of a pair (compare 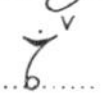 *endless* and  *needless*).

Those same principles can be adapted to avoid similar clashes in phrases, and some examples of their use are given here. Many of the individual sub-principles are fundamental ones that should be used from the very beginning of training (e.g. the distinction by vocalization between such pairs as  *of me* and  *of him*).

It does not follow that, because two outlines have the same form, they will necessarily clash. In some instances, context alone will indicate which of the pair is required. For example, whether *had not* or *do not* is appropriate will usually be apparent from the sense. On the other hand, at the beginning of a sentence, it might be helpful to vocalize a phrase such as  *we had not*, simply as an aid to transcription.

A good shorthand writer will generally know at once if there is a danger of confusion and will automatically make the necessary distinction. It is this sort of ability, or the lack of it, that demonstrates the thoroughness or otherwise of early training.

Context is always of some assistance in transcription, but there are occasions when  results can follow from not making distinctions such as those set out below.

### 1 Vocalization

When two outlines are identical except for the vowels, the obvious way to distinguish between them is to insert the vowel in one and leave the other unvocalized (though some writers may prefer to vocalize both):

 at last  at least

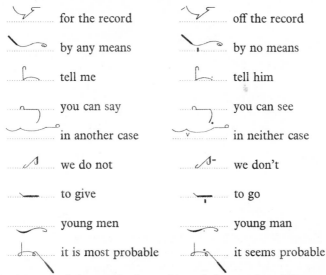

| | | | |
|---|---|---|---|
| for the record | | off the record | |
| by any means | | by no means | |
| tell me | | tell him | |
| you can say | | you can see | |
| in another case | | in neither case | |
| we do not | | we don't | |
| to give | | to go | |
| young men | | young man | |
| it is most probable | | it seems probable | |

In the case of the words *those, this* and *these*, rather different considerations apply. In the first place, it is sometimes possible (as set out in the very first section of this book) to raise or lower the first outline of a phrase in order to keep the one following also in its own position: *in those,* *in this,* *in these;* *with those,* *with this,* *with these.*

In other cases, vocalization is essential. *Those*, although it is a short form that does not normally take a vowel, takes $\bar{o}$; *this* (also a short form) is left unvocalized; *these* (not a short form) is vocalized in the normal way. Compare the following: *for those,* *for this,* *for these;* *to those,* *to this,* *to these.* (*Note.* Since *who* and *whom* normally follow only *those*, there is then no need to show the vowel— *for those who.*)

## 2 Disjoining

In the following examples, the full-length stroke is joined and the half-length one disjoined:

| | | | |
|---|---|---|---|
| I know | | I note | |
| we know that | | we note that | |

129

it may seem        it might seem

who can be        who could be

These are similar, but they involve pairs of phrases, of which one includes the word *not* and the other a negative prefix:

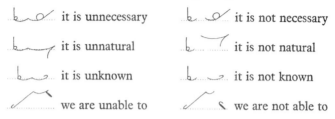

it is unnecessary      it is not necessary

it is unnatural      it is not natural

it is unknown      it is not known

we are unable to      we are not able to

In the groups of phrases illustrated in the previous two paragraphs, there is a definite pattern to be seen in the examples. The same principle should be applied to any similar pairs or adapted to any miscellaneous ones, as:

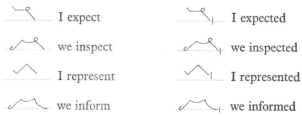

in all cases      in two cases

for the year      in the year

very well      very ill

## 3 Past tenses

In writing contracted forms singly, it is sometimes wise to make a distinction—notably between *subject* and *subjected*. The past tense may be indicated either by writing a small tick through the stroke ( ) or by placing a vertical tick at the side of the outline ( ). That distinction may also be used in phrases that contain such contracted forms. For the purpose of illustrating the principle, the vertical tick only is used in the examples that follow:

I expect      I expected

we inspect      we inspected

I represent      I represented

we inform      we informed

## 4 Miscellaneous

Some of these distinctions have been discussed in earlier sections in relation to the particular principles involved; others are simply sensible precautions against mistranscription:

| | | | |
|---|---|---|---|
| | I regard | | I regret |
| | my own | | mine |
| | in my own way | | in many ways |
| | in the course of time | | in course of time |
| | if there is | | for there is |
| | if it | | for it |
| | in other ways | | any other ways |
| | large part of | | large number of |
| | very much | | very large |
| | in a position | | in the position |
| | unable to | | enabled to |

The conversational forms such as ....... *don't* (compare ....... *do not*) are set out in section 11. The ones that follow do not involve halving; for the most part, they do not require an actual change of form—only the insertion of a vowel and/or a change of position:

| | | | |
|---|---|---|---|
| | we are | | we're |
| | you are | | you're |
| | he will | | he'll |
| | she will | | she'll |
| | they will | | they'll |
| | I am | | I'm |
| | I will | | I'll |

# Selected Phrases 17

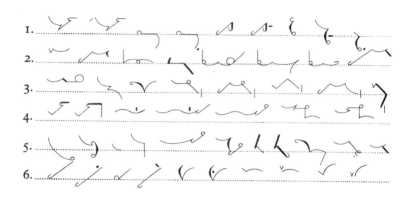

# Practice Material 17

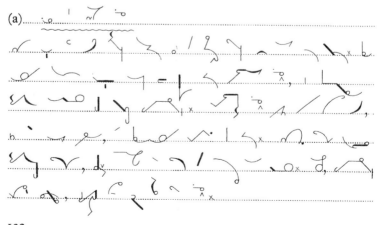

(b)

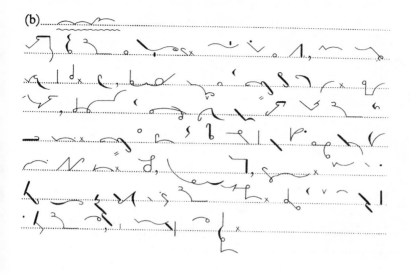

# Section 18

## Figures

### 1 General

(a) *Numbers below 10; phrases with* or

Although this is not a textbook on theory, it is worth repeating the suggested representation of numbers below 10. Apart from 8, the longhand figures could easily clash with shorthand outlines. Perhaps the most notable example is 6. It is quite plain that the shape of that longhand figure is very similar to the shorthand outlines that represent *it is*, *those*, *this* and *these*. In a sentence such as "It was those cases that were stolen", the hazard is self-evident. So it really is much safer to write one to nine (except eight) in shorthand and to use figures only for numbers 10 or above.

There are two ways of forming phrases when two numbers are linked by *or*. The first is to use omission, and the second is to use *ray* instead of *ar* to make the join:

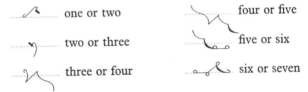

| | |
|---|---|
| one or two | four or five |
| two or three | five or six |
| three or four | six or seven |

Neither *eight or nine* nor *nine or ten* can satisfactorily be linked in either of the ways shown above—or, indeed, at all.

(b) *Numbers over 10*

When numbers reach hundreds, thousands or millions, figures are much the fastest way of representing them—and the danger of confusing them when they are in combination is minimal. However, if the numbers are round hundreds, thousands, hundreds of thousands or millions, it is sheer wasted effort (not to mention the possibility of *os* distorting into *6s*—or, of course, *6s* rounding themselves to look like *os*) to write in all the noughts.

Stroke *n* is used to represent *hundred*; stroke *ith* to represent *thousand*; stroke *m* to represent *million*. The signs may be used in combination with one another or with other outlines joined:

*Hundred*

300

300 people

600

600-plus

500

500 words

*Thousand*

2,000

2,000 people

4,000

4,000 men

7,000

7,000 times

(*Note.* Care should be taken to write *ith* clearly so that there is no possibility of confusion with the figure *1*. A high-speed device for the representation of *thousand* is a long oblique line, as *2,000*, *4,000*, *7,000*. This has the disadvantage that it is not often possible to join other outlines but the benefit of being very quick and easy to write. It is also easy to read back; and it does not require the careful formation that is needed for *ith*.)

*Million (and combinations)*

1m

100m

8m

8,000m

9m

900,000m

*Amounts of Money*

The outline for *pounds* will join to *n* for *hundred*; it requires the insertion of a circle between the *ith* and the *p* in amounts of thousands of pounds; it must be separated completely in amounts of millions of pounds:

£300          £1m

£2,000        £8,000m

(*Note.* Just as the long oblique stroke may be used for *thousands*, so in amounts of money it may be utilized—with the addition of a dot for

*pounds*: £2,000, £4,000, £7,000. This, again, is

a somewhat unorthodox short-cut, but it is very effective.)

It is also perhaps helpful to mention—though, again, it is not

strictly phrasing—that it is very useful to vocalize *pounds* ( ). As

the outline (*pence*) is so similar (though not halved), the insertion of the diphthong in *pounds* is a sensible precaution.


## 2 Dates

When representing years other than those in the present century, it is essential to write all the figures. It is unfortunate but necessary. Some people believe they will be able to remember which centuries go with which numbers, but in practice few, if any, are capable of such an effort of memory.

When writing any date that begins 19. ., it is possible (i) to write the four figures in full (e.g. *1965*), or (ii) to use an apostrophe, as one does in the longhand abbreviation of dates (e.g. '65). There are writers who advocate omitting the *19* and writing just the last two figures; but there are practical difficulties in that, too.

(*Note.* The oblique line suggested for use as *thousand* may also do duty

in this respect (e.g. ). There could be no confusion in the same device being used for both, because with dates there would be no preceding figure. Again, the real advantages are the speed of representation, the fact that there is no possibility of confusion with any other sign, and the sign itself does not call for absolute precision of penmanship.)


## 3 Fractions

Some fractions may be easily represented in shorthand (e.g. *one third*); others are more difficult, in that they are longer; but those are, generally speaking, the less common fractions. The most common ones—$\frac{1}{4}$, $\frac{1}{2}$ and $\frac{3}{4}$—are represented in the following way by many high-speed writers. The $\frac{1}{4}$ is an initially hooked stroke; the $\frac{1}{2}$ has a plain horizontal stroke; the $\frac{3}{4}$ takes the hook at the end of the stroke:

$$\overset{\llcorner}{2} \qquad 2\tfrac{1}{4}$$

$$\overline{9} \qquad 9\tfrac{1}{2}$$

$$\overline{4.} \qquad 4\tfrac{3}{4}$$

It is helpful to note that $\frac{1}{4}$ is the *first* of the group of three, and the hook is written *first* or *at the beginning*; the $\frac{1}{2}$ is in the middle and has no attachments; the $\frac{3}{4}$ is the *last* of the three, and the hook is written *last* or *at the end*.


## 4 Per cent

When *per cent* ( $\searrow$ ) follows a figure it may be represented by a simple stroke *p*. Should the combination *per cent per annum* occur, then the stroke may be repeated:

90⟍ 90%          5⟍⟍ 5% pa

40⟍ 40%          3⟍⟍ 3½% pa

# Selected Phrases 18

1.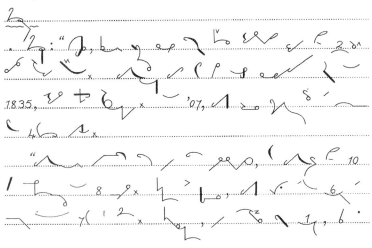
2.
3.
4.
5.
6.

# Practice Material 18

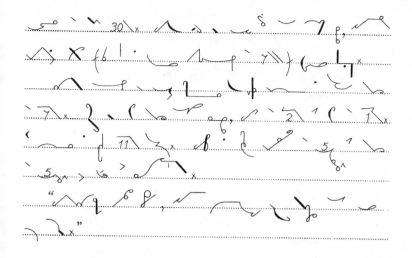

# Section 19

## *Specialist Vocabularies*

The previous sections have been concerned mainly with commercial material. However, some mention has been made of rather more specialized vocabularies. In this section, the basic and advanced principles already described are used, where applicable, to make phrases relevant to particular topics (e.g. *b* is intersected for *bank*; omission of a consonant by repetition is seen in *barium meal*; omission of a hook and intersection are used in *any other business*). However, sometimes the words represented in phrases by circles, hooks, intersections and omission are different from those to be found in the earlier sections.

It is worth referring, also, to the widespread use of initials, which in some instances make acronyms. In most circumstances, the easiest way of dealing with initials is to use lower-case longhand letters. They can be readily joined one to another and are much faster to write than capital letters. Examples are: BBC—*British Broadcasting Corporation*— *bbc* ; CCC—*Central Criminal Court*— *ccc* ; EEG—*electro-encephalogram*— *eeg* . An instance where an acronym is formed is *NATO*. In such circumstances, it may be better and quicker to write the full shorthand ( ⌐ ), rather than use the longhand letters.

Any selection of phrases that is intended to be representative of a particular kind of vocabulary must necessarily be limited. Careful study of the individual phrases under any of the various headings will reveal the principles that have been employed. It cannot be sufficiently stressed, however, that space does not permit the inclusion of other than sample phrases. In fact, the lists as such may be of more value to a freelance reporter, who may have to cover all these fields—and it is impossible to be an expert in everything. For the true specialist, a much deeper study of the individual subject is essential.

# Banking

advance against a life policy

bank giro

bank note

Barclaycard

base rate

bearer cheque

cancel the cheque

cash dispenser

certified cheque

cheque card

clearing house

crossed cheque

direct debit

Executor & Trustee Department

giro credit

investment management service

joint stock bank

last indorser

negotiable instrument

negotiable security

not negotiable cheque

paying-in slip

rate of exchange

refer to drawer

restrictive indorsement

specially indorsed

standing order

traveller's cheque

Treasury bills

without recourse

written authority of the drawer

# Company

annual general meeting

annual report

any other business

available for distribution

board of directors

cumulative preference shares

debenture stock

declaration of a dividend

| | | | | |
|---|---|---|---|---|
| | declare a dividend | | | paid-up capital of the company |
| | directors' report | | | preference dividend |
| | extraordinary general meeting | | | preference share-holders |
| | I am glad to move the adoption | | | preference shares |
| | in moving the adoption of the report and accounts | | | profit and loss account |
| | industrial relations | | | profit margin |
| | interim dividend | | | subsidiary companies |
| | managing director | | | to make a distribution |
| | ordinary dividend | | | turn to the balance sheet |
| | ordinary shareholders | | | turning to the profit and loss account |
| | paid-up capital | | | your directors |

## Correspondence and Commercial

| | | | | |
|---|---|---|---|---|
| | account sales | | | circular letter |
| | additional cost | | | discount for cash |
| | additional expense | | | I am directed to inform you |
| | advertising manager | | | I am directed to state |
| | at your earliest convenience | | | I am in receipt of your letter |
| | bill of exchange | | | I am instructed to inform you |
| | bill of sale | | | I am instructed to state |
| | by passenger train | | | I am requested to inform you |
| | by return of post | | | I have to acknowledge receipt of your letter |

142

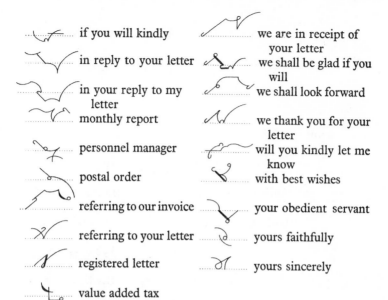

if you will kindly

we are in receipt of your letter

in reply to your letter

we shall be glad if you will

in your reply to my letter

we shall look forward

monthly report

personnel manager

we thank you for your letter

postal order

will you kindly let me know

referring to our invoice

with best wishes

referring to your letter

your obedient servant

registered letter

yours faithfully

value added tax

yours sincerely

## Electrical Engineering

alternating current

high resistance

amplitude modulation

high voltage

automatic gain control

induced current

cathode ray tube

induction coil

circuit diagram

intrinsic current

direct current

leakage current

discharge resistance

line time base

electrical engineer

low voltage

electro-magnetic waves

moving coil

field time base

primary cell

frequency modulation

primary coil

143

primary currents

secondary coil

secondary current

single phase

thermionic diode

## Government and Political

Act of Parliament

Agriculture, Fisheries and Food

at the first reading

at the second reading

at the third reading

cabinet meeting

chairman of committee

Chancellor of the Exchequer

Conservative Party

Department of the Environment

First Lord of the Treasury

Foreign and Commonwealth Office

freedom of the press

hon. and learned member

hon. gentleman

hon. member for Preston

House of Commons

House of Lords

Houses of Parliament

in the House of Commons

in the House of Lords

Labour Party

Leader of the House

Leader of the Opposition

Leader of the Party

Liberal Party

Member of Parliament

my hon. and gallant friend

my hon. friend

National Insurance Act

Parliamentary Committee

party leaders

Prime Minister

proportional representation

right honourable

right hon. gentleman

_..._ Secretary of State     _..._ social security

_..._ Secretary of State for Scotland     _..._ social security benefit

_..._ Secretary of State for Wales     _..._ supplementary benefit

## Insurance

_..._ annual premium     _..._ loan on the policy

_..._ automatic sprinklers     _..._ medical examination

_..._ bonus declaration     _..._ motor insurance

_..._ claim for compensation     _..._ no claim discount

_..._ consequential loss     _..._ personal accident insurance

_..._ damage by fire     _..._ personal injury

_..._ damage to premises     _..._ policies are declared void

_..._ Employers' Liability     _..._ policy is declared void

_..._ endowment assurance     _..._ proposal form received

_..._ fire insurance     _..._ quinquennial valuation

_..._ immediate benefit     _..._ registered number of the car

_..._ in full discharge of all claims     _..._ renewal of the policy

_..._ incombustible materials     _..._ responsibility of the company

_..._ industrial life assurance     _..._ surrender value

_..._ life policy

## Legal

_..._ articles of association     _..._ Chancery Division

_..._ Central Criminal Court     _..._ circumstantial evidence

| | | | |
|---|---|---|---|
| ⌐ℓₒ | counsel for the defence | ⌐ℓ | justice of the peace |
| ⌐ℓ | counsel for the defendant | | King's Bench |
| ⌐ℴ | counsel for the plaintiff | | King's Bench Division |
| ⌐ℴ | counsel for the prisoner | | King's Counsel |
| ⌐ℴ | counsel for the prosecution | | learned counsel |
| | Court of Appeal | | learned counsel for the defence |
| | Court of Appeal (Criminal Division) | | learned judge |
| | deed of assignment | | legal estate |
| | deed of settlement | | legal personal representative |
| | deed of transfer | | Lord Chancellor |
| | documentary evidence | | Lord Chief Justice |
| | documents of title | | magistrates' court |
| | examination-in-chief | | majority verdict |
| | Family Division | | marriage settlement |
| | grand jury | | may it please your Honour |
| | Habeas Corpus | | may it please your Lordship |
| | heirs, executors, administrators and assigns | | memorandum of association |
| | | | my learned friend |
| | heirs, executors, administrators or assigns | | Official Receiver |
| | | | originating summons |
| | High Court of Justice | | power of attorney |
| | judgment summons | | prima facie |

146

| | Queen's Bench | | trust funds |
| | Queen's Bench Division | | verdict for the defendant |
| | Queen's Counsel | | verdict for the plaintiff |
| | recognizance | | will and testament |
| | reversionary interest | | your Worship |

## Mechanical Engineering

| | automatic transmission | | injection moulding |
| | ball bearings | | internal combustion engine |
| | braking system | | metal fatigue |
| | civil engineer | | overhead valve |
| | coefficient of expansion | | oxy-acetylene welding |
| | combustion chamber | | potential energy |
| | consulting engineer | | pressure gauge |
| | control valve | | pressure release valve |
| | electro-motive force | | roller bearings |
| | exhaust valve | | rotary converter |
| | front-wheel drive | | self-tapping screw |
| | gear ratio | | sparking plug |
| | hydraulic press | | steam turbine |
| | hydro-elastic suspension | | vacuum pump |

## Medical

| | abdominal tumour | | angina pectoris |

| | | | |
|---|---|---|---|
| | bacillus tuberculosis | | obstructive jaundice |
| | barium meal | | orthopaedic surgeon |
| | blood pressure | | out-patient clinic |
| | blood transfusion | | peritoneal inflammation |
| | brain tumour | | pernicious anaemia |
| | cardio-vascular | | phenobarbitone |
| | circulatory system | | plastic surgery |
| | dislocation of the wrist | | presystolic murmur |
| | formaldehyde | | private practice |
| | fracture of the humerus | | radio-active iodine |
| | Grave's disease | | rheumatic fever |
| | hay fever | | salmonella infection |
| | heart disease | | secondary haemorrhage |
| | infant mortality | | semi-lunar valve |
| | intravenous injection | | thyroid cartilage |
| | jugular vein | | tonsillectomy |
| | lumbar puncture | | under the influence of drink |
| | mental deficiency | | vitamin deficiency |
| | muscular atrophy | | |

## Railway

| | | | |
|---|---|---|---|
| | area manager | | British Rail |
| | break down plant | | British Railways Board |

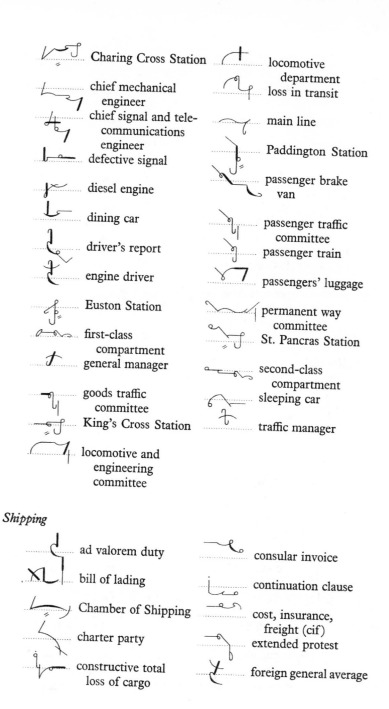

Charing Cross Station

chief mechanical engineer

chief signal and tele-communications engineer

defective signal

diesel engine

dining car

driver's report

engine driver

Euston Station

first-class compartment

general manager

goods traffic committee

King's Cross Station

locomotive and engineering committee

locomotive department

loss in transit

main line

Paddington Station

passenger brake van

passenger traffic committee

passenger train

passengers' luggage

permanent way committee

St. Pancras Station

second-class compartment

sleeping car

traffic manager

*Shipping*

ad valorem duty

bill of lading

Chamber of Shipping

charter party

constructive total loss of cargo

consular invoice

continuation clause

cost, insurance, freight (cif)

extended protest

foreign general average

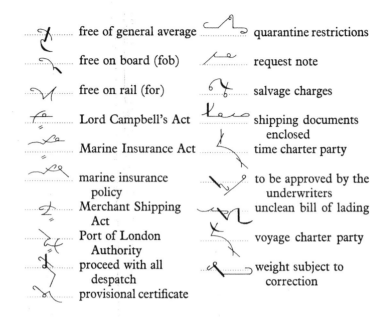

| | |
|---|---|
| free of general average | quarantine restrictions |
| free on board (fob) | request note |
| free on rail (for) | salvage charges |
| Lord Campbell's Act | shipping documents enclosed |
| Marine Insurance Act | time charter party |
| marine insurance policy | to be approved by the underwriters |
| Merchant Shipping Act | unclean bill of lading |
| Port of London Authority | voyage charter party |
| proceed with all despatch | weight subject to correction |
| provisional certificate | |

## Stockbroking

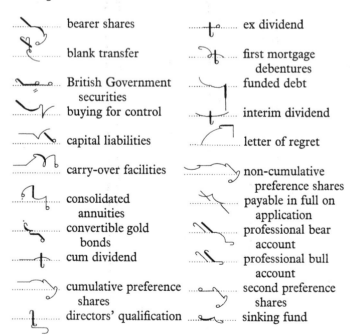

| | |
|---|---|
| bearer shares | ex dividend |
| blank transfer | first mortgage debentures |
| British Government securities | funded debt |
| buying for control | interim dividend |
| capital liabilities | letter of regret |
| carry-over facilities | non-cumulative preference shares |
| consolidated annuities | payable in full on application |
| convertible gold bonds | professional bear account |
| cum dividend | professional bull account |
| cumulative preference shares | second preference shares |
| directors' qualification | sinking fund |

...... sinking operations      ...... subscribed capital

...... special settlement      ...... surplus profits

...... Stock Exchange      ...... upward movement

...... stocks and shares      ...... yield per cent

# PART FOUR
# Alphabetical List

The list that follows is arranged in alphabetical order. It consists of examples of the principles set out in this book; but, it will be appreciated, no list can be exhaustive. However, if the various principles have been studied carefully, a writer coming across ⟨shorthand⟩ *have been* will find it relatively simple to build upon, as follows: ⟨shorthand⟩ *I have been,* ⟨shorthand⟩ *we have been,* ⟨shorthand⟩ *as we have been,* ⟨shorthand⟩ *I have been there,* ⟨shorthand⟩ *we have been there,* ⟨shorthand⟩ *as we have been there.* That means that six additional combinations have been formed from the basic phrase.

In the same way, many phrases may be extended by the addition of *to* or *of*—e.g. ⟨shorthand⟩ *give him* might become ⟨shorthand⟩ *to give him;* ⟨shorthand⟩ *yesterday morning* might become ⟨shorthand⟩ *of yesterday morning.*

Under 'O', the phrase ⟨shorthand⟩ *old age* appears. An obvious extension of that is *old age pensioner,* which can be achieved by using *p* as a special intersection: ⟨shorthand⟩. Under 'F', the phrase ⟨shorthand⟩ *first time* is given. Omission of *the* makes ⟨shorthand⟩ *for the first time* an acceptable derivative.

It will, therefore, be apparent that, while this list contains only some 3,000 individual phrases, by the application of the appropriate principles it is possible to make two or three times that number.

It is important to remember that some phrases may be represented in more than one way. Those below are shown in two forms. It is not a question of one being "right" and the other being "wrong". Either is acceptable, depending on how the spoken words are phrased. The shorthand phrasing should follow the natural pattern of speech:

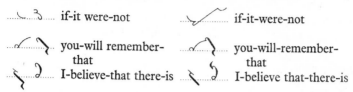

The most important point is that writers should not wait for a phrase that they *think* is going to be spoken. On hearing *in moving the adoption* . . ., a shorthand writer should represent those words at once. The rest of the phrase may be something that will join (for instance, *in moving the adoption . . . of the report and accounts—* ); it may, equally, be a combination wholly unsuitable for phrasing (e.g. *in moving the adoption . . . of the audited accounts and directors' report*).

able to agree

able to make

about the

above their

absolutely certain

absolutely sure

according to my

according to the

Act of Parliament

after a time

after he is (has)

after that

after the war

after they (them)

after we have

after which the

against us

agreed that

all classes

all directions

all friends

all great

all his (is)

all his interests

all his life

all his own

all his purposes

all mankind

all manner

all manner of ways

all matters

all means

all members

all my life

all my time

all one

all other classes

all our own

all over the country

all over the world

all parts

all persons

all places

all proceedings

all questions

all respects

all right

all situations

all sorts of

all states

all such

all that day

all that is necessary

all that one

all the matters

all the men

all the work

all the world

all the year round

all their own

all these circumstances

all these occasions

all these parts

all these questions

all these reasons

all this time

all those who are

all those who may be

all very well

all we can

all we want

all were (we are)

all you can

almost always

almost any

almost certain

| | | | |
|---|---|---|---|
| almost immediately | | and of the | |
| almost impossible | | and such | |
| almost undoubtedly | | and that they were | |
| already been | | and the Government | |
| also state | | and the rest | |
| always been | | and there were | |
| always excepting | | and they were told | |
| among the most | | and under the present circumstances | |
| among the same | | | |
| among themselves | | and we shall be pleased | |
| among those who have not | | another affair | |
| | | another instance | |
| among those who were | | another nation | |
| amongst them | | another opinion | |
| and after that | | another point | |
| and afterwards | | another question | |
| and have since | | another situation | |
| and I am | | another subject | |
| and I have the honour | | another time | |
| and I hope | | any business | |
| and I notice | | any more | |
| and I only | | any other | |
| and I take this | | any person | |
| and I took | | any word | |
| and I trust | | anything else | |
| and if it is to be | | anywhere else | |
| and if such | | apart from | |
| and if this is | | are not | |
| and if you will | | are not entitled | |
| and in all probability | | are you | |
| and in all the circumstances | | army and navy | |
| | | as a general rule | |
| and in my opinion | | as a result | |
| and in some cases | | as a rule | |
| and in some respects | | as compared (with) | |
| and in their | | as compared with last year | |
| and in this way | | | |
| and is (his) | | as directed | |

| | | | |
|---|---|---|---|
| as early as possible | | as long as necessary | |
| as far as | | as long as possible | |
| as far as can | | as long as they | |
| as far as may be | | as long as will | |
| as far as our | | as many as are | |
| as far as the | | as many as can be | |
| as far as usual | | as much as before | |
| as far as was | | as much as can be | |
| as far as will | | as much as ever | |
| as far as you can | | as much as it is | |
| as fast as | | as much as may | |
| as good as | | as much as our (are) | |
| as good as before | | as much as possible | |
| as good as ever | | as much as they | |
| as good as if | | as much as was | |
| as good as it | | as much as will | |
| as good as need be | | as much as your | |
| as good as possible | | as per | |
| as has been | | as promised | |
| as he is (has) | | as provided | |
| as he was | | as regards | |
| as if the most | | as satisfactory | |
| as in the case of | | as soon as convenient | |
| as is (his) | | as soon as possible | |
| as it certainly | | as soon as they were | |
| as it has not yet | | as soon as we have | |
| as it is | | as suggested | |
| as it really | | as the | |
| as it seems to me | | as this is | |
| as it sometimes was | | as to | |
| as it surely | | as to the | |
| as it was | | as usual | |
| as it were | | as we are | |
| as it will | | as we do not think | |
| as it would | | as we have not | |
| as little as possible | | as we have said | |
| as long as it is | | as we may | |
| as long as it may | | as we think there is | |

156

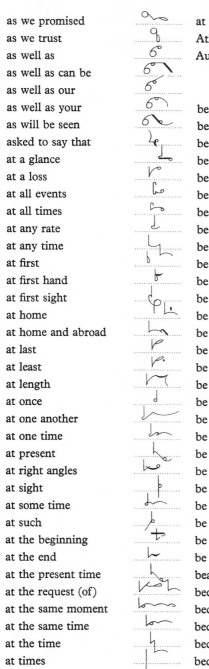

| | | |
|---|---|---|
| as we promised | | at your convenience |
| as we trust | | Atlantic Ocean |
| as well as | | Automobile Association |
| as well as can be | | |
| as well as our | | |
| as well as your | | be able to |
| as will be seen | | be assured |
| asked to say that | | be called upon |
| at a glance | | be certain |
| at a loss | | be clearly |
| at all events | | be considered |
| at all times | | be done |
| at any rate | | be gratified |
| at any time | | be greatly |
| at first | | be it so |
| at first hand | | be made |
| at first sight | | be pleased |
| at home | | be received |
| at home and abroad | | be said |
| at last | | be satisfied |
| at least | | be seen |
| at length | | be such |
| at once | | be supposed |
| at one another | | be sure |
| at one time | | be sure their (there) |
| at present | | be that as it may |
| at right angles | | be the case |
| at sight | | be their (there) |
| at some time | | be this |
| at such | | be thought |
| at the beginning | | be told that |
| at the end | | be your |
| at the present time | | bear in mind |
| at the request (of) | | because he |
| at the same moment | | because he could not |
| at the same time | | because he is (has) now |
| at the time | | because he was |
| at times | | because it cannot be |

| | | | |
|---|---|---|---|
| because it is | | best wishes | |
| because it was | | better and better | |
| because it will be | | better off | |
| because of | | better still | |
| because of their | | better than | |
| because such | | between his (us) | |
| because they have | | between our | |
| because this | | between them | |
| because we | | between which | |
| because we are | | bigger and bigger | |
| because we have | | board and lodging | |
| been able to | | bona fide | |
| been answered | | both sides | |
| been done | | bound to say | |
| been enabled | | boys and girls | |
| been known | | breach of faith | |
| been observed | | break up | |
| been received | | bring forward | |
| been required | | bring up | |
| been said | | British Isles | |
| been so | | British Medical | |
| been taken | | Association | |
| been told | | British Museum | |
| been understood | | British Rail | |
| before him | | British Railways Board | |
| before his | | British ships | |
| before my (me) | | broken up | |
| before the war | | business experience | |
| before us | | business letter | |
| before you | | business man | |
| being the case | | but can | |
| being the same | | but may | |
| believe that | | but one | |
| best of my recollection | | but so | |
| best of our ability | | but such | |
| best possible | | but surely | |
| best time | | but tell | |
| best way | | but that | |

158

| | |
|---|---|
| but their (there *or* they are) | by people |
| but they will | by permission |
| but this | by reason (of) |
| but we have received | by several |
| but we have taken | by some means |
| but we may | by some other means |
| but when | by something |
| but whenever | by such |
| but whether | by that |
| but would | by the Chairman |
| but you will have | by the Government |
| by all means | by the House |
| by any means | by the means |
| by as many | by the same |
| by certain | by the way |
| by circumstances | by their |
| by considering | by their means |
| by every | by their own |
| by far the least | by this |
| by far the most | by this nation |
| by far the worse | by this time |
| by him | by those who are |
| by his (us) | by those who are not |
| by his own | by which it appears |
| by his own statement | by which it can |
| by it | by which it has (is) |
| by its (itself) | by which it may |
| by its means | by which it seems |
| by land and sea | by which it would |
| by many | by which many |
| by me (my) | by which means |
| by means of | by which you |
| by myself | by you |
| by no means | by your |
| by one | by your own |
| by our | by your request |

159

| | | | |
|---|---|---|---|
| call attention to the matter | | cause and effect | |
| call that | | certain amount | |
| called upon | | certain circumstances | |
| came to the conclusion | | certainly been | |
| can be found | | certainly not | |
| can be said | | Chief Superintendent | |
| can be seen | | Church of England | |
| can become | | City of Manchester | |
| can do | | City of Norwich | |
| can have | | City of Westminster | |
| can it | | civil servant | |
| can it appear | | Civil Service | |
| can it be | | civil war | |
| can it bring | | civilized world | |
| can never | | clearly shown | |
| can only assume | | come forward | |
| can you have | | come to the conclusion | |
| cannot be | | comes forward | |
| cannot be considered | | Commander-in-Chief | |
| cannot be said | | Common Market | |
| cannot be there (their) | | considerable time | |
| cannot become | | Constitution of the United States | |
| cannot do | | consumers' association | |
| cannot expect | | cost of production | |
| cannot make | | could be | |
| cannot receive | | could have | |
| cannot regard | | could have been | |
| cannot say | | could have done | |
| cannot see | | could never | |
| cannot take | | could nevertheless | |
| car park | | could not be | |
| care of | | could not be the case | |
| carried on | | could not have | |
| carried on their | | could they | |
| carried out | | could you have | |
| carry on | | country town | |
| Catholic religion | | courts of law | |

160

| | |
|---|---|
| custom houses | door to door |
| | during the month |
| dear sirs | during the war |
| depend upon it | |
| depend upon us | each of them |
| did not | each other |
| did not know | each was |
| difference of opinion | early closing |
| directly or indirectly | East and West |
| distinctly understood | East Indies |
| do assure | Ecclesiastical Court |
| do not | electric light |
| do not be | Electricity Board |
| do not entirely | enclose herewith |
| do not know | end of next week |
| do not necessarily | end of the month |
| do not say | England and Wales |
| do not see | English language |
| do not understand | enter into |
| do not wish | ever been |
| do so | ever since |
| do something | every appearance |
| do sometimes | every consideration |
| do such | every day |
| do that | every direction |
| do they | every morning |
| do this | every one |
| do you mean to say | every other |
| do you mean to suggest | every station |
| do your | everywhere else |
| does appear | existing circumstances |
| does he | expect to receive |
| does it | expression of opinion |
| does not | extremely sorry |
| does nothing | |
| does one | fact of the matter |
| does that | fair and reasonable |
| does this | family life |

| far and wide | | for his interest | |
|---|---|---|---|
| farther than (on) | | for his opinion | |
| faster and faster | | for his own | |
| favourable circumstances | | for his part | |
| | | for his purpose | |
| fellow members | | for his sake | |
| few more | | for instance | |
| few weeks | | for it will be | |
| few words | | for many | |
| fewer than | | for me | |
| first aid | | for months | |
| first and foremost | | for my friends | |
| first class | | for my own sake | |
| first-hand information | | for no one | |
| first rate | | for one | |
| first time | | for perhaps | |
| five or six | | for possibly | |
| five pound note | | for sale | |
| following points | | for services rendered | |
| following words | | for several weeks | |
| for (a) consideration | | for several years | |
| for a few days | | for shipment | |
| for a long time | | for some considerable time | |
| for a moment | | | |
| for a time | | for some reason or other | |
| for another | | for some time past | |
| for even | | for some years | |
| for ever | | for something | |
| for fear | | for such matters | |
| for further particulars | | for the account | |
| for he was | | for the first time | |
| for he would have the | | for the Government | |
| for he would not | | for the main | |
| for his account | | for the management | |
| for his advantage | | for the moment | |
| for his appearance | | for the most part | |
| for his country | | for the pleasure | |
| for his information | | for the present | |

| | | | |
|---|---|---|---|
| for the record | | from every | |
| for the sake of | | from first to last | |
| for the same reason | | from him | |
| for the work | | from its | |
| for the year | | from many | |
| for their opinion | | from month to month | |
| for their satisfaction | | from some cause | |
| for their support | | from the beginning | |
| for them (they) | | from the fact that | |
| for there has been | | from the first | |
| for there is | | from the other | |
| for there were | | from the place | |
| for they were | | from time immemorial | |
| for this | | from time to time | |
| for this bill | | from us | |
| for this country | | from whom | |
| for this time | | from year to year | |
| for those who | | from you | |
| for us | | from your | |
| for we are told | | full particulars | |
| for we had | | fully qualified | |
| for we were | | further consideration | |
| for where | | further instructions | |
| for which we are obliged | | further than (on) | |
| for which you are | | future advantage | |
| for whom | | future time | |
| for you | | | |
| for your consideration | | General Election | |
| for your information | | general manager | |
| foreign affairs | | general secretary | |
| foundation stone | | generally speaking | |
| four or five | | generation to generation | |
| free of charge | | get rid of | |
| freehold property | | get rid of their | |
| from among | | give him | |
| from as many | | give me | |
| from beginning to end | | give the matter | |
| from certain | | good deal | |

163

| | | | |
|---|---|---|---|
| good enough | | has been received | |
| good fortune | | has he | |
| good many | | has it | |
| good men | | has it ever been | |
| great advantage | | has not been | |
| great affairs | | has that | |
| great applause | | has this | |
| Great Britain | | have also | |
| great danger | | have another | |
| great difference | | have become | |
| great difficulty | | have been | |
| great events | | have been able to | |
| great expense | | have been expecting | |
| great interest | | have been given to understand | |
| great opportunities | | | |
| great pleasure | | have been known | |
| great respect | | have been received | |
| great value | | have been told | |
| greater number of | | have believed | |
| greater part (of) | | have calculated | |
| greater than | | have called | |
| | | have closely | |
| | | have come to the conclusion | |
| had been | | have decided | |
| had not | | have demanded | |
| had not been | | have done | |
| had not been there | | have endeavoured | |
| had not known | | have every | |
| had their | | have found | |
| had you | | have frequently | |
| half a million | | have great hopes | |
| hard and fast | | have greatly | |
| hard and fast rule | | have heard | |
| hardly likely | | have indeed | |
| has been | | have it | |
| has been considered | | have just | |
| has been issued | | have just been | |
| has been made | | | |

164

| have known | | having heard | |
|---|---|---|---|
| have lately | | he can | |
| have likewise | | he cannot be | |
| have long | | he has (is) | |
| have mentioned | | he has (is) never | |
| have much pleasure | | he has (is) not | |
| have never been | | he has received | |
| have no doubt | | he must be | |
| have no objection | | he seems | |
| have no time | | he seems to be able to | |
| have not been able to | | he should be | |
| have one | | he was | |
| have only | | he was there | |
| have only just | | he will be | |
| have perhaps | | he will never | |
| have pleasure | | he will not be | |
| have possibly | | he would have | |
| have probably | | he would have been | |
| have said | | he would make | |
| have seen | | he would not | |
| have sent | | hear, hear | |
| have shown | | hear you | |
| have some | | heart and soul | |
| have sometimes | | heavy expenses | |
| have spoken | | Her Majesty | |
| have such | | her own | |
| have suggested | | here and there | |
| have supposed | | high pressure | |
| have taken | | high state of | |
| have the honour | | hinder us | |
| have their (there) | | his is (has) | |
| have this (these *or* those) | | His Majesty | |
| have thought | | his own | |
| have to be | | his own interests | |
| have told | | history of the world | |
| have tried | | hither and thither | |
| have understood | | Home Office | |
| have we | | Home Secretary | |

| | | | |
|---|---|---|---|
| honourable and gallant member | | I am going to speak to you | |
| hon. senator | | I am greatly | |
| House of Commons | | I am in doubt | |
| House of Representatives | | I am instructed | |
| | | I am most | |
| house to house | | I am never | |
| how can | | I am not | |
| how can there be | | I am not quite sure | |
| how can we | | I am persuaded | |
| how far | | I am pleased | |
| how long | | I am quite sure | |
| how much | | I am ready | |
| how the | | I am sorry | |
| how the matter | | I am sorry to say | |
| human being | | I am sure you | |
| human character | | I am therefore | |
| human kind | | I am told | |
| human life | | I am truly | |
| human mind | | I am very sorry | |
| human nature | | I assure you | |
| human race | | I became | |
| Hyde Park | | I become | |
| | | I believe | |
| | | I bequeath | |
| I agree | | I call | |
| I agree with | | I can assure you | |
| I am | | I can never | |
| I am able to | | I can tell you | |
| I am afraid | | I cannot expect | |
| I am also | | I consider | |
| I am aware | | I could not have | |
| I am certain that you will | | I criticized | |
| | | I dare | |
| I am concerned | | I dare not | |
| I am convinced | | I dare say | |
| I am extremely sorry | | I desire | |
| I am free | | I did not | |

| | | | |
|---|---|---|---|
| I do not say | | I suppose | |
| I do not see | | I take | |
| I do not think that | | I take this | |
| I do not wish it to be | | I tell him | |
| I feel | | I thank | |
| I feel sure | | I think it is necessary | |
| I gave | | I think so | |
| I had | | I think that we | |
| I have already been | | I think there is | |
| I have already seen | | I thought that | |
| I have no objection | | I told him | |
| I have suggested | | I took | |
| I hope that | | I tried | |
| I hope there will be | | I trust you will | |
| I intended | | I understood | |
| I know nothing | | I want | |
| I know there is | | I was never | |
| I like | | I was there | |
| I may say | | I was under the impression | |
| I mentioned | | | |
| I must | | I will endeavour | |
| I must not be | | I will tell you | |
| I must now | | I wish it were not | |
| I must take | | I would | |
| I need hardly say | | I would like to know | |
| I need not say | | if convenient | |
| I observed | | if he | |
| I presume | | if he can | |
| I promise | | if he has been | |
| I propose | | if he were | |
| I referred | | if he will be | |
| I remember | | if he would | |
| I see no objection | | if his | |
| I shall never | | if it | |
| I shall take | | if it becomes | |
| I shall therefore | | if it did not | |
| I speak | | if it has (is) | |
| I spoke | | if it has (is) never | |

167

| | | | |
|---|---|---|---|
| if it is convenient | | if you require | |
| if it is found | | if you would | |
| if it please | | in a few days | |
| if it possibly | | in a large number of cases | |
| if it prove | | | |
| if it was | | in a month's time | |
| if it were | | in a position | |
| if it would | | in accordance with | |
| if necessary | | in addition to the | |
| if only | | in all cases | |
| if possible | | in all matters | |
| if that is not the case | | in all parts of the country | |
| if that is possible | | | |
| if the matter | | in all probability | |
| if the present | | in another case | |
| if there/their | | in another sense | |
| if there is one | | in another world | |
| if there is one thing | | in any affair | |
| if there were | | in any case | |
| if therefore | | in any instance | |
| if they | | in any position | |
| if they are | | in any respect | |
| if this country | | in any situation | |
| if this gentleman | | in any way | |
| if this is the case | | in appearance | |
| if those who are | | in as far as | |
| if we are | | in charge | |
| if we are unable to | | in (the) circumstances | |
| if we believe | | in committee | |
| if we have seen | | in comparison with the | |
| if we may | | in conclusion | |
| if we take | | in conformity with | |
| if we understand | | in connection with their | |
| if you are successful | | in consequence (of) | |
| if you can | | in control | |
| if you like | | in effect | |
| if you mean | | in every way | |
| if you please | | in fact | |

168

| | | | |
|---|---|---|---|
| in favour | | in other words | |
| in him | | in our opinion | |
| in his | | in person | |
| in his account | | in place of the | |
| in his case | | in possession | |
| in his day | | in question | |
| in his face | | in reality | |
| in his hands | | in relation to the | |
| in his interest | | in reply to the | |
| in his opinion | | in some | |
| in his own case | | in some cases | |
| in his own interest | | in some countries | |
| in his own way | | in some respects | |
| in his own words | | in some way | |
| in his time | | in spite of | |
| in it | | in spite of the fact | |
| in its own | | in succession | |
| in its place | | in such matters | |
| in judgment | | in such places | |
| in many | | in that day | |
| in many cases | | in that direction | |
| in me | | in that matter | |
| in mine | | in that way | |
| in more | | in the account | |
| in most | | in the case of | |
| in most cases | | in the circumstances | |
| in my own | | in the contract | |
| in neither case | | in the country | |
| in nine cases out of ten | | in the course of | |
| in no case | | in the dark | |
| in one form or another | | in the direction | |
| in one word | | in the early part (of) | |
| in order that the | | in the event (of) | |
| in order to | | in the first place | |
| in order to be sure | | in the form (of) | |
| in other directions | | in the House | |
| in other respects | | in the land | |
| in other ways | | in the manner (of) | |

169

| | |
|---|---|
| in the matter (of) | in this world |
| in the meantime | in those |
| in the morning | in time |
| in the name (of) | in vain |
| in the nature of things | in which event |
| in the ordinary course of events | in which it has been |
| | in which it is |
| in the ordinary way | in which there are |
| in the other | in which we have been |
| in the past | in which you are engaged |
| in the same way | |
| in the second place | in which you require |
| in the shape of | in your last letter |
| in the street | in your letter |
| in the truth | inasmuch as |
| in the words | including their |
| in the world | income tax |
| in the year | instead of the |
| in their case | into effect |
| in their own case | into most |
| in their own interests | into that |
| in their place | into their |
| in their statements | into this country |
| in their view | is as (his) |
| in themselves | is it |
| in these | is it likely |
| in these circumstances | is it not |
| in these words | is it possible |
| in this | is it the |
| in this affair | is it true |
| in this age | is it worth while |
| in this century | is necessary |
| in this city | is no doubt |
| in this difficulty | is not one |
| in this direction | is not only |
| in this manner | is not this |
| in this place | is that the wisest |
| in this respect | is the |

| | | | |
|---|---|---|---|
| is the matter |  | it is no longer | |
| is the most | | it is not logical | |
| is this | | it is not the first time | |
| is to | | it is nothing | |
| it appears to me | | it is now | |
| it can have | | it is one | |
| it certainly | | it is (has) only just | |
| it has been done | | it is plain | |
| it has been said | | it is possible | |
| it has been suggested | | it is rather | |
| it has not been | | it is ready | |
| it is a well-known fact | | it is really | |
| it is absolutely necessary | | it is seen | |
| it is admitted | | it is shown | |
| it is agreed | | it is so | |
| it is also | | it is something | |
| it is as (his) | | it is sometimes | |
| it is believed | | it is such | |
| it is better than | | it is sufficient | |
| it is calculated | | it is suggested | |
| it is certainly not | | it is taken | |
| it is clearly | | it is the case | |
| it is considered | | it is this | |
| it is difficult | | it is thought | |
| it is equal | | it is time | |
| it is expected | | it is to be | |
| it is found | | it is true | |
| it is generally | | it is truly | |
| it is impossible | | it is unnecessary | |
| it is intended | | it is well known | |
| it is interesting | | it is worth while | |
| it is just | | it is worthy | |
| it is just possible | | it is written | |
| it is most | | it is wrong | |
| it is most probable | | it is your own | |
| it is needed (indeed) | | it is yours | |
| it is never | | it looks | |
| it is no doubt | | it makes | |

| | | | |
|---|---|---|---|
| it may not be | | ladies and gentlemen | |
| it may seem | | laid down | |
| it may well be | | large measure | |
| it means | | large number | |
| it must | | large number of cases | |
| it must certainly | | large number of men | |
| it seems impossible | | large part (of) the | |
| it seems probable | | larger and larger | |
| it should not be | | last few days | |
| it sometimes | | last moment | |
| it sometimes seems | | last month | |
| it stands to reason | | last time | |
| it surely | | last week | |
| it was impossible | | last year | |
| it was known | | later than (on) | |
| it was nothing | | latter part (of) | |
| it will also be found | | law court | |
| it will appear | | leading article | |
| it will be found | | learned friend | |
| it will be impossible | | learned gentleman | |
| it will be observed | | learned member | |
| it will be seen | | leasehold property | |
| it will never be | | leave the matter | |
| it will not be | | leave us | |
| it will take | | legal representative | |
| it would appear | | let us | |
| it would be something | | let us be | |
| it would have been | | let us consider | |
| it would only | | let us have | |
| | | let us hope | |
| just a few | | let us know | |
| just after | | let us remember | |
| just as | | let us say | |
| just been | | let us see | |
| just enough | | let us try | |
| just finished | | let you have | |
| just in time | | like to have | |
| just now | | little advantage | |

172

| little consideration | | many of those who | |
| little more | | many of you | |
| little more than | | many people | |
| little time | | many persons | |
| live wire | | many such | |
| local board | | many things | |
| logical conclusion | | many think that | |
| long before | | mark of respect | |
| long enough | | may also | |
| long life | | may as well | |
| long one | | may be able to | |
| long since | | may be called | |
| long standing | | may be considered | |
| long time ago | | may be made | |
| long way | | may be used | |
| longer and longer | | may bring | |
| longer than | | may certainly | |
| looking forward | | may consider | |
| Lord Mayor | | may greatly | |
| Lord President | | may have been | |
| Lord Provost | | may mention | |
| loss of life | | may never | |
| lower and lower | | may not | |
| lunch time | | may not be | |
| | | may only | |
| | | may probably | |
| Magna Carta | | may serve | |
| major part (of) | | may sometimes | |
| make it clear | | may therefore | |
| make their way | | may you | |
| make way | | Medical Board | |
| manner in which | | medical corps | |
| many feel | | medical examination | |
| many have | | medical journal | |
| many instances | | medical student | |
| many more | | Member of Parliament | |
| many nations | | Members of Parliament | |
| many of these | | men and women | |

| | | | |
|---|---|---|---|
| middle ages | | much more than | |
| middle classes | | much obliged | |
| minor complaint | | much pleasure | |
| modern times | | musical instrument | |
| Monday afternoon | | must admit | |
| Monday evening | | must also | |
| Monday morning | | must appear | |
| Monday next | | must ask | |
| more and more | | must bring | |
| more certain | | must consider | |
| more favourable | | must do | |
| more freely | | must expect | |
| more frequent | | must generally | |
| more frequently | | must have | |
| more important | | must have been | |
| more likely | | must make | |
| more or less | | must mean | |
| more than another | | must necessarily | |
| more than their | | must needs be | |
| more time | | must never | |
| most anxious | | must not | |
| most certainly | | must not be | |
| most difficult | | must prove | |
| most excellent | | must receive | |
| most important | | must say | |
| most likely | | must see | |
| most men | | must take | |
| most natural/ly | | must try | |
| most necessary | | must undoubtedly | |
| most probable/y | | my dear friend | |
| Mr. and Mrs. | | my dear Miss Brown | |
| Mr. Chairman | | my good friend | |
| Mr. Mayor | | my hon. and learned | |
| Mr. President | | friend | |
| Mr. Speaker | | my kind regards | |
| much as | | my life | |
| much as it is | | my love | |
| much more | | my mind | |

174

| | | | |
|---|---|---|---|
| my noble and learned friend | | neither of them | |
| my noble and rev. friend | | never been | |
| my noble and right rev. friend | | never said | |
| | | never was | |
| my noble friend | | new ships | |
| my only fear | | new year | |
| my opinion | | news agency | |
| my own | | next month | |
| my own account | | next week | |
| my own advantage | | no advantage | |
| my own belief | | no alternative | |
| my own case | | no appearance | |
| my own circumstances | | no doubt | |
| my own conclusion | | no fewer than | |
| my own endeavours | | no instance | |
| my own experience | | no interest | |
| my own feeling | | no knowledge | |
| my own interest | | no less than | |
| my own part | | no longer than | |
| my own sake | | no more than | |
| my own sentiments | | no necessity | |
| my own things | | no objection | |
| my own time | | no part | |
| my own understanding | | no such | |
| my partner | | no time | |
| my son | | no worse than | |
| my time | | noble lord | |
| | | nor can | |
| national affairs | | nor did | |
| nearer and nearer | | nor do | |
| need appear | | nor have | |
| need be | | nor in | |
| need necessarily | | nor is it | |
| need never | | nor is this | |
| need not | | nor need | |
| needless to say | | nor such | |
| neither instance | | nor was | |
| | | nor were they | |

nor will

north, south, east and
   west

not absolutely

not been

not enough

not even

not excepting

not generally

not in vain

not less

not less than

not more

not necessarily

not necessary

not one

not only

not possible

not so

not such

not that

not these

not this

not those

not understood

not we

nothing else

nothing is less

nothing more

notwithstanding such

notwithstanding that

notwithstanding the fact
   that

now and then

number of

of advantage

of as few

of as many

of course this is (has)

of every one

of great advantage

of her own

of him

of his own

of his time

of itself

of many things

of one of his

of several

of some

of some importance

of such matters

of such men

of the case

of the matter

of the way

of this Bill

of this century

of this country

of this mentality

of those who are

of us

of very great

of which it must be said

of which we are now

of your letter

of yours

off the record

official receiver

old age

old man

old men

on account of many

on account of the

on account of your

| | | | |
|---|---|---|---|
| on every | | one of our | |
| on his behalf | | one of the most | |
| on his face | | important | |
| on his own | | one of these days | |
| on his part | | one or other | |
| on many occasions | | one or two | |
| on me (my) | | one point (pound) | |
| on most | | one thing | |
| on one | | one understands | |
| on one side | | one way | |
| on some | | one word | |
| on such occasions | | only been | |
| on the committee | | or not | |
| on the one hand | | or perhaps | |
| on the other hand | | or rather | |
| on the other side of the | | or some other | |
| on the present occasion | | or something | |
| on the subject | | or sometimes | |
| on this occasion | | or surely | |
| on this question | | or there | |
| on this side | | ordinary circumstances | |
| on your part | | other circumstances | |
| once again | | other classes | |
| once more | | other people | |
| once or twice | | other questions | |
| one and all | | other side | |
| one another | | other times | |
| one another's interest | | other way | |
| one by one | | ought never | |
| one cannot expect | | ought not | |
| one instance | | ought not to | |
| one knows not | | ought not to be | |
| one man | | ought not to have | |
| one may | | ought to be considered | |
| one month | | ought to be made | |
| one more | | ought to have | |
| one must | | our own | |
| one of his | | our part | |

| | | | |
|---|---|---|---|
| out of | | political advantage | |
| out of doors | | political association | |
| out of the question | | political opinion | |
| out of the way | | political power | |
| out of there (their) | | post office | |
| over and above | | postage stamp | |
| over and over again | | postal services | |
| over them | | present advantage | |
| over there (their) | | present age | |
| over which the | | present and future | |
| owing to the fact | | present instance | |
| | | present question | |
| Pacific Ocean | | present state of things | |
| part and parcel | | present time | |
| part of | | President of the United States | |
| pass away | | price lists | |
| past year | | Prime Minister | |
| pen and ink | | Prince of Wales | |
| per annum | | Princess of Wales | |
| per cent | | printing press | |
| per day | | private and confidential | |
| per dozen | | public house | |
| per head | | public library | |
| per kilogramme | | public meeting | |
| per month | | public service | |
| perfectly clear | | purchase agreement | |
| perfectly satisfactory | | purchase money | |
| personal experience | | | |
| personal representative | | quite agree | |
| personal service | | quite certain | |
| Pitman writer | | quite correct | |
| please give me | | | |
| please inform | | rate of | |
| please let us know | | reason to suppose | |
| please make arrangements | | reasonable time | |
| plenty of | | right or wrong | |
| point of view | | Right Rev. Bishop | |

| | | | |
|---|---|---|---|
| Roman Catholic | | shall take | |
| round and round | | shall there (their) | |
| rules and regulations | | shall there be | |
| | | she can | |
| satisfactory conclusion | | she cannot | |
| satisfactory manner | | she did not | |
| satisfactory result | | she had | |
| say so | | she has (is) | |
| second time | | she has been | |
| secondary education | | she has (is) not | |
| secondary schools | | she has nothing | |
| seeing you | | she may | |
| seems to have | | she never | |
| seems to have been | | she says | |
| seems to me | | she seems | |
| sending you the | | she shall | |
| sent to you | | she sometimes | |
| set apart | | she was | |
| set aside | | short space of time | |
| set forth | | short time | |
| set off (of) | | short time ago | |
| set out | | shorthand writer | |
| several times | | shorthand writing | |
| shall be glad | | should be considered | |
| shall be served | | should be said | |
| shall do | | should become | |
| shall endeavour | | should feel | |
| shall expect | | should have seen | |
| shall give | | should have told you | |
| shall go | | should know | |
| shall make | | should never | |
| shall most likely | | should nevertheless | |
| shall never | | should not be made | |
| shall not be able to | | should only | |
| shall receive | | should these | |
| shall require | | should this | |
| shall say | | should those | |
| shall see | | should understand | |

| | | | |
|---|---|---|---|
| shoulder to shoulder | | so that we may | |
| side by side | | so to speak | |
| significant fact | | so was | |
| signs of the times | | so well (will) | |
| since it | | so would | |
| since no doubt | | so you are | |
| since nothing | | so you must | |
| since that | | solar system | |
| since that time | | some account | |
| since they | | some amount | |
| since this is the case | | some care | |
| since which | | some consideration | |
| Sir Isaac Pitman | | some man | |
| Sir James | | some may | |
| six months | | some means | |
| six months ago | | some measure | |
| six or seven | | some men | |
| smaller than | | some months | |
| so are | | some of them | |
| so are they | | some of you will | |
| so be it | | probably remember | |
| so called | | some one | |
| so do | | some one or other | |
| so far | | some other | |
| so far as the | | some people | |
| so forth | | some people seem to | |
| so good | | imagine | |
| so good as to | | some perhaps | |
| so has (is) | | some probability | |
| so he | | some reason or other | |
| so it seems | | some reference | |
| so little | | some regard | |
| so long as | | some seem inclined | |
| so may | | some such | |
| so must | | some time | |
| so much as | | some time ago | |
| so soon as | | some time or other | |
| so sure | | some time since | |

| | | | |
|---|---|---|---|
| something has been said | | such has no doubt | |
| something like | | such has (is) not | |
| something to his advantage | | such have been | |
| | | such is his | |
| somewhere else | | such is not the case | |
| sort of | | such is the case | |
| South Africa | | such matters | |
| spare time | | such men | |
| speaking from memory | | such principles | |
| special circumstances | | such was | |
| St. Paul | | such were | |
| standard of living | | such will | |
| state of affairs | | such would | |
| steam engine | | | |
| steps are being taken | | take care | |
| still more | | take care of | |
| stronger than | | take charge | |
| struggle for existence | | take courage | |
| such a manner | | take down | |
| such a manner as to | | take exception | |
| such a plan | | take into account | |
| such and such | | take it for granted | |
| such are they | | take out | |
| such as are | | take part (of) | |
| such as can | | take(n) place | |
| such as can be | | take some time | |
| such as he | | take steps | |
| such as it is | | take such | |
| such as may | | take that | |
| such as must be | | take the case (of) | |
| such as need not | | take the chair | |
| such as that | | take the place (of) | |
| such as this | | take them | |
| such as were | | taken into account | |
| such cases | | taken part | |
| such considerations | | takes away | |
| such has been | | takes notes | |
| such has (is) never | | taking part | |

| | | | |
|---|---|---|---|
| technical college | | that is possible | |
| technical terms | | that is so | |
| tell him | | that is thought | |
| tell it | | that is to be | |
| tell me | | that is to say | |
| tell such | | that is understood | |
| tell that | | that is where | |
| tell them | | that is worse | |
| tell us | | that is worth | |
| tell you | | that it has (is) | |
| tell your | | that it may be | |
| tells me | | that it must be done | |
| tells us | | that may be | |
| than the other | | that perhaps | |
| thank you | | that plan | |
| that circumstance | | that question | |
| that day | | that such | |
| that difficulty | | that supposition | |
| that does | | that the country | |
| that does not | | that the directors | |
| that has been | | that the matter | |
| that has (is) never | | that there are | |
| that has not been | | that there are several | |
| that he can have | | that there must be | |
| that he has been | | that there should be | |
| that he may | | that there should have been | |
| that he must be | | | |
| that is a question | | that they are | |
| that is another | | that they were | |
| that is intended | | that this affair | |
| that is it | | that this was | |
| that is necessary | | that those nations | |
| that is not the | | that thought | |
| that is nothing | | that time | |
| that is now | | that was | |
| that is one | | that way (we) | |
| that is one point | | that we are able to | |
| that is only | | that we could not | |

| | | | |
|---|---|---|---|
| that we have made | | there is no objection | |
| that which will be | | there is no occasion | |
| that will do | | there is no one | |
| that you should not be | | there is no reason why | |
| their measures | | there is no subject | |
| their own | | there is no such | |
| their reasons | | there is nothing | |
| there and then | | there is now | |
| there are | | there is occasion | |
| there are a great many | | there is only | |
| there are not | | there is possibly | |
| there are now | | there is something that | |
| there are persons | | there is sometimes | |
| there are several | | there is still | |
| there are some | | there is undoubtedly | |
| there are those | | there may not | |
| there can be | | there must | |
| there cannot | | there must have been | |
| there certainly | | there seemed | |
| there did not | | there sometimes | |
| there do not | | there was another | |
| there does not | | there were | |
| there has been | | there will have been | |
| there has (is) never | | there would have been | |
| there has never been | | these circumstances | |
| there has not been | | these gentlemen | |
| there has (is) now | | these questions | |
| there have been | | these things | |
| there is another fact | | they appear | |
| there is as much | | they are certain that | |
| there is (has) certainly | | they are expecting | |
| there is hardly | | they are not | |
| there is little | | they are perhaps | |
| there is little prospect | | they are possibly | |
| there is much | | they are required | |
| there is need | | they believe | |
| there is (has) never | | they care | |
| there is no doubt | | they did not | |

183

| | | | |
|---|---|---|---|
| they do | | think you may | |
| they do not | | this account | |
| they have been | | this advantage | |
| they have not seen | | this afternoon | |
| they have received | | this appears | |
| they made | | this bill | |
| they may | | this cannot | |
| they may not be | | this circumstance | |
| they must | | this city | |
| they must not be | | this conclusion | |
| they probably | | this could not | |
| they said that | | this country | |
| they speak | | this day | |
| they state | | this department | |
| they suppose | | this did not | |
| they that | | this difficulty | |
| they themselves | | this discussion | |
| they think that | | this does | |
| they thought | | this done | |
| they were | | this evening | |
| they will not | | this generally | |
| they would | | this had | |
| think he | | this has become | |
| think him | | this has been | |
| think it | | this has never | |
| think me (my) | | this has no doubt | |
| think perhaps | | this has not | |
| think that | | this has nothing to do | |
| think their (there) | | this has the | |
| think them (they) | | this he | |
| think there has (is) | | this instance | |
| think there has been | | this intention | |
| think there has (is) | | this interest | |
|    never | | this is done | |
| think there has (is) not | | this is intended | |
| think they may | | this is it | |
| think this | | this is known | |
| think this is | | this is never | |

| | | | |
|---|---|---|---|
| this is no doubt | | those accounts | |
| this is no time | | those advantages | |
| this is not | | those appearances | |
| this is not the case | | those countries | |
| this is nothing | | those days | |
| this is now | | those did not | |
| this is the case | | those difficulties | |
| this is where | | those discussions | |
| this knowledge | | those have | |
| this letter | | those nations | |
| this month | | those parts | |
| this morning | | those places | |
| this need | | those that | |
| this no doubt | | those things | |
| this notice | | those which | |
| this now | | those which we are now | |
| this one | | those which we have | |
| this one thing | | those who have | |
| this opinion | | those who were | |
| this part | | though he | |
| this party | | though it | |
| this period | | though that | |
| this place | | though their (there) | |
| this point | | though then | |
| this purpose | | though there had | |
| this question | | though there has been | |
| this reason | | though there has (is) not | |
| this statement | | though there was | |
| this subject | | though there were | |
| this thing | | though there will | |
| this time | | though these (this) | |
| this vote | | though they | |
| this was | | thought he | |
| this week | | thought it | |
| this will | | thought that | |
| this will not | | thought them | |
| this world | | thought this | |
| this would | | thought we were | |

| | | | |
|---|---|---|---|
| three months | | to believe | |
| three or four | | to belong | |
| through as many | | to blame | |
| through his interest | | to bring the matter | |
| through his own | | to call | |
| through it | | to certain | |
| through many | | to choose | |
| through me | | to do | |
| through their | | to every | |
| through their own | | to expect | |
| through you | | to give | |
| throughout the world | | to give an expression of opinion | |
| till his | | to give and take | |
| till his own | | to go | |
| till it can | | to have the same | |
| till my | | to have their | |
| till some | | to hear (here) | |
| till such | | to Her Majesty's Government | |
| till that | | | |
| till their | | to him | |
| till then | | to his advantage | |
| till these (this) | | to his knowledge | |
| till they | | to His Majesty's Government | |
| till we | | | |
| till you | | to his memory | |
| to a certain extent | | to his notice | |
| to a great degree | | to his own advantage | |
| to a great extent | | to his own interest | |
| to account | | to its (itself) | |
| to advantage | | to make application | |
| to agree with you | | to make the most | |
| to amount | | to make way | |
| to appear | | to many of them | |
| to assure the | | to me | |
| to be made | | to mention | |
| to be served | | to my part | |
| to become | | to one another | |
| to behave | | | |

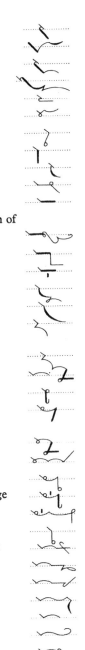

186

| | | | |
|---|---|---|---|
| to our friends | | too many | |
| to prevent | | too much | |
| to propose | | too short | |
| to receive | | too true | |
| to satisfy | | towards it | |
| to say a few words | | towards one another | |
| to seek | | towards that | |
| to serve | | towards this | |
| to some extent | | trade union | |
| to speak to you | | twelve months | |
| to state | | two or three | |
| to such | | two years ago | |
| to suppose | | | |
| to take | | unable to consider | |
| to that which you | | unable to find | |
| to the account of | | under no | |
| to the amount | | under no circumstances | |
| to the best advantage | | under such | |
| to the truth | | under the circumstances | |
| to their | | under these | |
| to these | | circumstances | |
| to these institutions | | under this | |
| to these places | | under way | |
| to this | | under which | |
| to those | | Union Jack | |
| to try | | United Kingdom | |
| to us | | United States of | |
| to which you can | | America | |
| to whom | | up to date | |
| to your | | up to the present | |
| tomorrow afternoon | | up to the time of writing | |
| tomorrow evening | | upon their | |
| tomorrow morning | | upon us | |
| too far | | upon which | |
| too great | | | |
| too late | | valuable time | |
| too little | | various parts | |
| too long | | very bad | |

187

| | | |
|---|---|---|
| very best | | was meant |
| very certain | | was mentioned |
| very far | | was necessary |
| very first | | was never |
| very freely | | was no doubt |
| very frequently | | was not |
| very good | | was not aware |
| very late | | was not found |
| very likely | | was nothing |
| very many of them | | was received |
| very much more | | was said |
| very pleased indeed | | was seen |
| very rare | | was so |
| very serious | | was some |
| very short | | was sometimes |
| very short time | | was soon |
| very similar | | was there |
| very soon | | was therefore |
| very sure | | was to be received |
| very true | | was understood |
| very well | | waste of time |
| vice versa | | ways and means |
| viva voce | | we are afraid |
| vote of thanks | | we are entitled |
| | | we are glad |
| was another | | we are in receipt of your letter |
| was as | | |
| was as much | | we are not |
| was better | | we can do |
| was done | | we can only be |
| was expected | | we can say that |
| was he | | we could not be |
| was issued | | we did |
| was it right | | we did not |
| was it so | | we do (had) |
| was known | | we do not |
| was lately | | we do not think |
| was made | | we find |

188

we had not

we have already said

we have already referred

we have also

we have no time

we have some

we hope

we may be certain

we may be sure

we must

we must not

we propose

we regret

we regret to state

we reply

we shall be glad to
receive

we shall expect

we shall not

we shall require

we spend

we take

we then

we think there is

we thought

we trust that you will

we were

we were not

we will

we would

we would be

we would not be

we write

well aware

well-known

well-known fact

well then

well there is

were not

were you

West End

West End of London

West Indies

what amount

what can be done

what cannot

what do

what do not

what does

what in the world

what is called

what is it

what is the matter

what is the reason

what it has (is)

what matter

what must

what position

what was

what was the matter

what were the

what would be

what you

whatever be

when do

when do you go

when does

when he was there

when these

when this

when those

when we are (when
were)

when we are not

when we are told

when you

| | | | |
|---|---|---|---|
| whenever he | | which is understood | |
| whenever his | | which it is understood | |
| whenever it may | | which made | |
| whenever that | | which makes | |
| whenever there has (is) | | which many | |
| whenever they | | which may be | |
| whenever this | | considered | |
| where were | | which may not | |
| wherever there is | | which must be | |
| whether certain | | which one | |
| whether it is | | which perhaps | |
| whether it is or not | | which probably | |
| whether it will be | | which represent-ed | |
| whether or not | | which seems | |
| whether there are | | which seems to me | |
| whether they | | which some | |
| whether we believe | | which was necessary | |
| which appear | | which we may have | |
| which are not | | which will not | |
| which could not be | | which you may require | |
| which do (had) | | while there is | |
| which has never been | | while they | |
| which has (is) no doubt | | while this | |
| which has (is) now | | who are never | |
| which has (is) possibly | | who are they | |
| which has (is) your | | who cannot | |
| which have been | | who come | |
| which have the | | who could not | |
| which (of) have their | | who has done | |
| which is believed | | who has (is) it | |
| which is certainly | | who has (is) the | |
| which is intended | | who has (is) this | |
| which is known | | who have not | |
| which is no | | who said | |
| which is not only | | who seems to me | |
| which is often | | who suppose that | |
| which is sometimes | | who were | |
| which is thus | | will be able to make | |

| | |
|---|---|
| will be glad to know | without his |
| will be the case | without his knowledge |
| will have | without it |
| will have no alternative | without one |
| will have their | without such |
| will it be | without that |
| will it not | without their |
| will not | without them |
| will only be | without this |
| will perhaps | without which |
| will probably | witness-box |
| will their (there) | word for word |
| will therefore | words a minute |
| will you | working classes |
| will you please | working man |
| with advantage | worse and worse |
| with each | worth while |
| with equal advantage | would be something |
| with equal effect | would expect |
| with equal satisfaction | would give |
| with one | would go |
| with one another | would happen |
| with one thing | would have been |
| with reference to it | would hope |
| with reference to that | would indeed |
| with reference to this | would interest |
| with regard to him | would it not be |
| with regard to the | would know |
| with the present | would mention |
| with the same | would never |
| with this country | would not have |
| with this end in view | would not have been |
| with those whom | would possibly |
| with us | would rather |
| with which we have sent | would receive |
| with you | would say |
| within necessary | would see |
| without doubt | would understand |

| | |
|---|---|
| would you | |
| would your | |
| wrong way | |
| | |
| year ago | |
| year by year | |
| year since | |
| years ago | |
| years and years | |
| year's lease | |
| years of age | |
| year's rent | |
| yes, if you please | |
| yes or no | |
| yes, sir | |
| yesterday afternoon | |
| yesterday evening | |
| yesterday morning | |
| yield per ton | |
| you are not | |
| you are only | |
| you are requested | |
| you can | |
| you cannot | |
| you make | |
| you may as well | |
| you may consider | |
| you may rest assured | |

| | |
|---|---|
| you must (most) certainly | |
| you must consider | |
| you must have been | |
| you refer | |
| you should have seen | |
| you were not | |
| you will consider | |
| you will not | |
| you will probably agree | |
| you will remember | |
| you will say | |
| you will see | |
| you would | |
| young man | |
| young men | |
| young person | |
| your board | |
| your instructions | |
| your letter | |
| your own | |
| your reply | |
| yours faithfully | |
| yours sincerely | |
| yours truly | |
| | |
| zero rated | |

# PART FIVE

## Longhand of Selected Phrases and

## Practice Material

### SELECTED PHRASES 1

1. we-shall, we-shall-be, we-shall-be-glad, I-shall, I-shall-be, I-shall-be-glad, we-think, we-think-you-are, I-think, I-think-you-are
2. you-are, that-you-are, you-may, if-you-may, I-think-you-may, we-think-you-may, I-think-you-may-be, we-think-you-may-be
3. we-are, we-are-glad, we-are-glad-that, we-are-glad-that-you-are, we-are-glad-that-you-can, we-are-glad-that-you-will
4. we-are-sorry, we-are-not, we-are-sure, we-are-pleased, we-regret, we-regret-that, we-know, we-know-that
5. it-is(-has), it-is(-has)-not, it-has-not-been, which-is(-has), which-is(-has)-not, which-has-not-been, that-is(-has), that-is(-has)-not, that-has-not-been, he-is(-has), he-is(-has)-not, he-has-not-been
6. we-have, we-have-done, I-have, I-have-done, they-have, they-have-done, we-have-not-done, I-have-not-done, they-have-not-done

---

7. for-your, for-your-letter, for-your-letters, for-your-receipt, for-your-receipts, for-years(-yours), for-several-years, for-many-years
8. we-must, you-must, they-must, she-must, he-must, we-may, he-may, they-may, she-may, you-may
9. as-to, as-it, as-it-is(-has), as-it-is(-has)-not, as-it-has-not-been, as-it-seems, as-it-seems-to-be, there-seems, there-seems-to-be, he-seems, he-seems-to-be

10. dear-sir, dear-sirs, dear-madam, dear-Miss-Brown, yours-truly, point-out, to-offer-you, we-have-pleasure, we-have-much-pleasure
11. no-doubt, there-is, there-is-no-doubt, there-was, there-was-no-doubt, there-are, there-are-several, no-more, there-is-no-more
12. good-enough, it-is-enough, long-enough, long-time, very-long-time, very-good, very-bad

---

13. we-are-told, we-are-told-that, we-are-informed, we-are-informed-that, inform-you, this-afternoon, this-evening
14. for-you, have-you, if-you, for-you-are, if-you-are, of-you, to-you, tell-you, to-tell-you, we-can-tell-you
15. last-year, last-years, two-years, three-years, three-months, two-months, those-days, in-those-days, these-days, in-these-days
16. and-yet, and-no-one-else, and-for-this-reason, and-we-have-seen, to-make, to-take, to-tell, to-run, to-jump, to-laugh, to-win
17. we-can, can-we, we-do(-had), do-we, we-can-have, can-we-have, we-can-see, can-we-see
18. of-much, of-which, of-each, with-much, with-which, with-each, that-those, that-this, that-these, in-those, in-this, in these

## PRACTICE MATERIAL 1

(a) *Letter from travel agent*

Dear-Madam, We-thank-you for-your-letter, and-we[10]-have-pleasure in-sending-you-the brochure for-which-you[20] asked. You-will-see that-it-has-been designed to[30]-give-you as-much information as-possible about-the holidays[40] that-we-can offer.

There-is-no-doubt that some[50] tours are more popular than others, but-you-must realize[60] that a good-deal depends on-each person's own taste.[70] We-can-tell-you, however, that-the-country to-which[80] most people seem to-want to-go is Spain. During[90]-the-last three-years, we-have-had more bookings for[100] our three holidays in Spain than for any-where-else. The[110] first of-these three is-the one numbered 6 in[120]-the-brochure; the second one is number 9; and-the[130] third is-the one numbered 14. It-is for-you[140] to decide which-combination of-places appeals to-you most.[150] All-the holidays last for two weeks, as there-seems[160]-to-be very-little demand for a longer or shorter[170] time.

All-the prices quoted in-the-brochure include-the[180] cost of-the flight and-full board at a first[190]-class hotel. If-you wish, you-may pay a small[200] deposit now, the balance then becoming due two-months before[210]-the date of-your departure. You-are, of-course, at[220]-liberty to pay-the full amount later, but in-that[230] event we-could-not guarantee a place for-you on[240]-the tour of-your choice. Yours-truly, (247)

## (b) *Motoring*

It-is-not at-all unusual in-these-days for[10] people to-have cars. They-may-have a small vehicle,[20] they-may-have a bigger one—and-there-are some[30]-people who, it-seems, cannot-be-content unless they-have[40]-the very biggest kind available.

There-are many-ways of[50] paying for-such a car. For-instance, one method is[60]-to pay by cash, but-that does-not appeal to[70]-most buyers. A second possibility is-to pay a little[80] each-month until the whole amount has-been repaid. This[90]-may take two-years or three-years, depending on-the[100] value of-the vehicle. In-the-case of-such regular[110] sums being paid, it-is a very-good idea to[120]-make-arrangements through a bank for-the-money to-be[130] paid direct. There-can-then be no-doubt that-the[140]-money has-been sent, as there-may-be, for-example,[150] if a cheque is sent through-the post. You-can,[160] of-course, make-sure that-you have proof of-delivery[170] by using-the recorded delivery service.

You-are-now the[180] owner of a motor-car. If-you think-that-is[190]-the end of-the-matter, you-are very mistaken. There[200]-is tax and-insurance to pay; there-is-the cost[210] of-regular servicing; there-is-the cost of petrol and[220] oil.

For-all this expenditure you have achieved-the doubtful[230] pleasure of-going out on-the roads to-join-the[240] thousands of other cars and lorries. The next-time you[250]-are stuck in a traffic-jam, it-would-be interesting[260] to-think back to-the day you collected your first[270] motor-car.                (272)

## (c) *The Common Market*

The Common-Market is-the partnership of-several countries in[10]-certain areas of-trade and-industry. To-begin with, it[20]-was France and-Germany who-were to-join together. But[30]-they said-that it-would-be open to any European[40] country to enter-the-Community also. At-that-time, four[50] other countries applied, and-they became members. A good-many[60] years-later, the Six, as-they-were-called, asked-us[70] in-Britain if-we wished to-join. We-did do[80]-so, together-with two of-the other countries to-whom[90] invitations were-made.

New posts had to-be-made so[100]-that our interests in particular fields, such-as finance, could[110]-be dealt-with by a minister who had special knowledge[120] on-that subject. Our-own ministers meet those from-the[130] other member countries; and-these meetings are-known as-the[140] Council of-Ministers. There-is, in-addition, a European Parliament.[150] It-must-be-consulted on any major issues that-may[160] arise.

As no-doubt you-would expect, there-are times[170] when actions of-the-Council of-Ministers may-be in[180]-question. For-this-reason, there-is a Court of-Justice[190] to-make decisions on any-such-matters.    (197)

# SELECTED PHRASES 2

1. pay-the, by-the, can-the, give-the, for-the, if-the, have-the, think-the, in-the, are-the, weigh-the

2. at-the, add-the, try-the, may-the, lay-the, which-the, touch-the, say-the, was-the, show-the, enjoy-the

3. address-the, makes-the, pass-the, choose-the, says-the, face-the, influence-the, raise-the, lose-the, guess-the, thinks-the

4. much-the, much-the-same, in-the-same, in-the-same-way, for-the-same, for-the-same-year, to-take-up-the, by-the-same, by-the-same-means

5. in-the-year, for-the-year, over-the-year, over-the-same, at-the-same, at-the-same-place, at-the-time, at-the-end, at-the-next, during-the-next

6. in-the-course, in-the-course-of-the, in-the-meantime, take-the-matter, give(n)-the-matter, all-over-the-country

---

7. of-the, to-the, on-the, but-the, with-the, when-the, what-the, would-the, how-the, why-the, that-the, beyond-the, and-the

8. I-have-the, I-have-not-the, I-have-had-the, I-have-not-had-the, I-think-the, I-think-that-the, I-think-that-you-will, I-think-that-you-are, I-see-the, I-wish-the

9. I-know, I-know-that, I-know-that-it-is(-has), I-know-that-it-is(-has)-not, I-took, I-took-the, I-took-the-matter, I-shall, I-shall-be

10. I-wish, I-was, I-say, I-see, I-feel, I-presume, I-call, I-raise, I-draw, I-play, I-glance

11. I-am, I-may, I-can, I-cannot, I-cannot-see, I-will, I-will-be, I-ran, I-went, I-trust, I-believe-that

12. you-will, you-will-be, you-are, you-can, you-can-be, you-could-not, you-could-not-be, you-may, you-may-be

---

13. if-you, if-you-will, if-you-will-be, if-you-are, if-you-can, if-you-can-be, tell-you, do-you, have-you

14. are-you, to-let-you, to-let-you-know-the, to-let-you-have, to-let-you-have-the, can-you, to-give-you, to-make-you, to-take-you

15. with-you, when-you, what-you, would-you, would-you-take, to-agree-with-you, when-you-think, what-you-do, would-you-go, to-go-with-you, to-take-with-you

16. how-are-you, I-know-that-you, I-know-that-the, you-can-say, you-must, I-must, you-mean, I-mean

17. that-he, that-he-is(-has), that-he-is(-has)-not, I-know-that-he, I-know-that-he-is(-has), I-know-that-he-is(-has)-not, I-think-he-is(-has), I-think-he-will, if-he-is(-has), if-he-is(-has)-not

18. he-will, if-he-will, he-is(-has), when-he-is(-has), he-can, if-he-can, he-says, that-he-says, he-seems, if-he-seems

# PRACTICE MATERIAL 2

### (a) *Company report*

I-am-going to ask-you now to-turn to[10]-the-accounts, and, as-to-the directors' statement, you-will[20]-have received a copy of-that already. From-the document[30] we-sent-you, it-will-be-seen that-we-have[40] given-you all-the information that-is available about-the[50] prospects in-the-year ahead. Regarding-the results for-the[60]-year as shown in-the-accounts, I-am-sure that[70]-you-will-understand that at-the-end of-the period[80] we-had to-give-the-matter of-further expansion very[90]-careful thought. You-can-see that-we-decided to-make[100]-the transfer of-funds in-these accounts, and-I-trust[110]-that-you-will-approve of-that course.

You-will-be[120]-sorry to-hear that Mr-Brown has-been unable-to[130] take-the-matter of-the merger any-further. I-know[140]-that-he-has done everything that-he possibly could, and[150] you-would probably wish me to-thank-him for-his[160] efforts in-the-course-of-the negotiations. I-believe-that[170]-the several meetings lasted many hours, and he-has travelled[180] all-over-the-country to-attend them. At-the-time,[190] it-seemed a very-good idea, but I-regret to[200]-tell-you that-the-terms we put-forward have-not[210]-been agreed.

It-is proposed to-let-you-know-the[220] final decision of-the-directors as-to-the dividend at[230]-the-next meeting. The date of-that will-be announced[240] at-the-end of-the proceedings. In-the-meantime, you[250]-are invited to-address any-questions you-may-have to[260]-the-chairman.

(262)

### (b) *Letter to conference secretary*

Dear-Sir, You-wrote to-me recently asking about-the[10] possibility of-our press officer coming to-address-the-Conference[20] that-you-are planning within-the-next two-months. He[30]-says that-he-can attend, as-he-is expecting to[40]-be in-the-same area at-the-time of-the[50]-Conference.

He-has asked-me to-let-you-have-the[60] outline of-what-he intends to say, and-this I[70]-am-enclosing. He-seems to-think that-the talk can[80]-be-made to-cover much-the-same ground as-he[90] dealt-with on-the previous occasion, but he-will make[100]-sure that all-the-information he uses is topical. If[110]-you-will let-me-know what-you think of-this,[120] I-can pass on to-him without-delay the decision[130] you-make.

I-think-he-has made-the necessary bookings[140] at-the hotel; and-I-assume you-will-be paying[150] his expenses, as-before. He-will himself send-you-the[160] bill from-the hotel and-one for-the fee on[170]-which-you have agreed.

I-take-this opportunity of-wishing[180]-you every success with-the-Conference. Yours-truly,

(188)

197

## (c) *Biography*

When-you hear-the name Walt Disney, you-may-think[10] of-the cartoon animals that-he created. There-is-no[20]-doubt that-he-was very famous for-them, for he[30]-seemed to-make-the characters so human. You-would-not[40]-be surprised to know-that-he always liked to-draw[50]-the animals that-he-saw about-the countryside. The first[60] money that-he earned was from a sketch that-he[70]-made of a horse.

In-the-course-of-his life,[80] he had many difficulties. Over-the-years when-he was[90]-not doing very-well, you might think-that-he would[100]-have become very depressed. When-he began one-company and[110]-that failed, you-would perhaps expect him to-give-up;[120] but he did-not. In-the-years that followed, he[130] tried to-make a success of-the ideas that-he[140] had. At-that-time, however, his work was-not appreciated.[150] It-is generally believed that-he began to-rise to[160]-the top when-he introduced the character of-Mickey Mouse,[170] who-is-now getting on in years.

If-you take[180]-the-matter of-money on its-own, Disney made a[190] lot from-the popularity of-Mickey. In-much-the-same[200]-way, he earned a good-deal from Snow White. You[210]-must realise, however, that what-he-was making then had[220] to-make-up for-all-the losses over-the-years.[230]

You-can-see, therefore, that-he worked hard and, now[240] that-he-is dead, the results of-his labours still[250] bring enjoyment to-thousands.

(254)

## SELECTED PHRASES 3

1. it-can-be-seen, it-will-be-seen-that, in-those-days, in-these-days, please-inform, we-notice-that, you-will-have-seen, in-these-times
2. these-matters, this-man, please-note-that, it-is-difficult, in-some, in-some-other, in-some-other-way
3. please-make, please-give-him, please-accept, it-is-really, it-is-impossible, it-is-rarely, it-seems-to-be, it-seems-to-me
4. at-the-same, in-the-same, with-the-same, to-the-same, for-the-same, over-the-same, do-the-same, much-the-same, all-the-same
5. with-his(-us), when-is(-has), what-is(-has), when-is(-has)-it, what-is-it, to-go-with-his(-us), to-agree-with-his(-us), what-is(-has)-the, when-is(-has)-the, when-is-the-matter
6. in-his, in-his-opinion, in-his-view, in-his-interests, it-is(-has), is-it, which-is(-has), which-is(-has)-not, it-has-been, it-has-not-been, which-has-been, which-has-not-been

7. as-to, as-to-the, as(-has)-the, as-much, as-much-as, as-far-as, as-far-as-the, as-early-as, as-long-as, as-fast-as, just-as
8. as-good-as, as-quickly-as, as-can-be-seen, as-they-said, as-he-is(-has), as-he-is(-has)-not, as-we-believe, as-we-believe-that, as-we-believe-that-the
9. to-us(-his), of-us(-his), in-us(-his), for-us(-his), from-us(-his), help-us(-his), to-give-us, let-us, let-us-say, let-us-see, against-us
10. I-can-say-that, we-can-say-that, asked-to-say-that, to-say-a-few-words, I-would-like-to-say-a-few-words, if-you-can-say-a-few-words, I-have-to-say-that, we-have-to-say-that
11. at-once, upon-us, depend-upon-us, medical-association, Automobile-Association, health-association, consumers'-association, Scottish-Association
12. as-per, as-per-the, as-produced, as-tried, as-promised, as-contrasted, as-directed, as-compared, as-compared-with-the, as-compared-with-last-year, as-compared-with-the-previous

---

13. in-which-it-has-been, if-it-is(-has)-not, from-its, I-do-not-think-it-is-necessary, I-know-there-is(-has), I-know-there-is(-has)-not, I-do-not-think-there-is(-has), to-render-us, hinder-us
14. last-time, last-week, past-year, past-few-years, past-few-days, just-received, best-time, best-time-of-life, amongst-others
15. most-important, to-take-steps, we-must-take-steps, I-trust-that, I-trust-that-you-will, we-trust-this-is-not, very-pleased-indeed, we-are-very-pleased-indeed
16. we-must-not, we-must-not-be, we-must-say, we-must-say-that, you-must-say, West-End, West-End-of-London, West-Indies
17. past-few-weeks, almost-impossible, we-must-ask-you, past-experience, at-the-last-moment, it-is-most-important, last-month
18. your-last-letter, in-your-last-letter, dear-sir, dear-sirs, yours-truly, yours-faithfully, chairman's-speech, yours-sincerely

## PRACTICE MATERIAL 3

(a) (i) *Memo from Office Manager to Despatch Department*

We-have-just-received a letter from a client in[10]-the West-End-of-London. He-was expecting delivery of[20]-his order last-week, but it-has-not-yet arrived.[30] This-is-not-the first-time that-he-has-been[40] faced with-the-same situation; but, as-far-as I[50]-can-tell from what-is already known, it-seems-to[60]-me that-his-complaint is almost-impossible to justify. I[70]-trust-that-you-will at-once take-steps to-find[80] out what-is-the position and let-me-know as[90]-soon-as you-can. (94)

## (ii) Memo from Despatch Department to Office Manager

I-have-to-say-that I-am-surprised that-this[10] customer in-the West-End has written to-us again[20] and-that-he-has-complained in-much-the-same terms[30] as-he-has done before. It-has-not-been possible[40] always to-deliver his goods as-quickly-as he-would[50] like. In-the past-few-years, it-has-been in[60]-his-interests to-accept-commitments and depend-upon-us to[70]-supply what-he-has needed. I-think-there-is-no[80]-doubt that, as-usual, he-has turned against-us because[90]-the goods did-not reach-him as-fast-as he[100] expected.

In-these-days, delivery times are-not as-early[110]-as they used to-be; but I-know-there-is[120]-nothing we-can-do to-improve them. As-this-man[130] is-not satisfied with-the delivery offered, and-as-it[140]-is almost-impossible to-give-the kind-of service he[150] wants, is-it not time for-us to-terminate-the[160] account? (161)

## (iii) Letter to customer

Dear-Sir, We-have-to-say-that your-letter of[10]-last-week has given-us some distress. We-must-say[20] that-we at-once took-steps to investigate your-complaint,[30] as-is our policy.

It-seems that-the last-time[40] you-made such a complaint the difficulty arose in-the[50]-same-way. You-will-not in-the-circumstances get from[60]-us the assurance you seek. You-must-see that-such[70] a demand is beyond what-is normally expected and-is,[80] for-that reason amongst-others, almost-impossible to comply with.[90]

As-the-matter stands, we-think-there-is-no-point[100] in-our-continuing to-do business, as-we-believe-that[110]-the differences between-us cannot-be resolved. Yours-faithfully, (119)

## (b) Vice-chairman's speech

As-promised, copies of-the chairman's-speech have-been sent[10]-out in-the-last-week. As-can-be-seen from[20]-it, the results are as-good-as we-expected, especially[30] as-compared-with-last-year's.

I-would-like-to-say[40]-a-few-words, however (as-the chairman him-self is-not[50] with-us), about-the suggestion made in-the past-few[60]-days that-we-send a representative to-the political-association[70] in-this-town. This-is intended, of-course, to-give[80]-us local support, but I-have-been asked-to-say[90]-that such a connection would hinder-us-considerably. We-must[100]-take-steps of-this-kind with great care, and-this[110]-is-not-the best-time for-us to-do-so.[120]

As-far-as-the staff are-concerned, it-has-not[130]-been an easy year for-them, and-I-am-sure[140] you-will-agree-with-us that-the bonus should-be[150] increased to five per-cent for-the-year. (158)

The minister said-that in-his-view it-was up[10] to-each one-of-us to-do as-much-as[20] we-can as-fast-as we-can. In-his-opinion,[30] it-was most-important, as that-was-the only way[40] in-which-the difficulties of-the past-few-years could[50]-be offset. He-continued: "The people of-this-country depend[60]-upon-us as-long-as we-do what-is right.[70]

"I-know-there-is action being taken to hinder-us,[80] but-we-shall at-once take-steps.to control-the[90] groups responsible. It-seems to-us that in-these-days[100] we-are facing an almost-impossible task. However, it-will[110]-be-seen-that we-are doing as-much-as we[120]-can for as-many-as we-can.

"I-do-not[130]-think-it-is-necessary for-me to-do more-than[140] point to-the opinion poll-conducted on-the last-day[150] of-last-month. As-to-the suggestion that our showing[160] in-the-same period is-not as-good-as that[170] of-the party that preceded us, this-is-not so.[180] In-fact, our-own results—as-compared-with-the ones[190] they achieved over-the-same length of-time—are very[200]-good indeed." (202)

## SELECTED PHRASES 4

1. as-we-can, as-we-can-be, as-we-can-be-there, as-we-can-see, as-we-can-tell, as-we-have, as-we-have-been, as-we-have-seen, as-we-have-seen-that

2. as-we-have-said, as-we-have-told-you, as-we-know, as-we-know-that, as-we-know-that-you-will, as-we-may, as-we-are, as-we-feel, as-we-felt

3. as-we-do, as-we-think, as-we-think-you-may, as-we-think-you-should, as-we-think-you-should-be, as-we-think-you-will, as-we-hope, as-we-hope-that, as-we-hope-that-you-are, as-we-say

4. as-we-shall, as-we-shall-be, as-we-shall-not, as-we-shall-not-be, as-we-shall-not-be-there, as-we-wish, as-we-had, as-we-had-been, as-we-took, as-we-went

5. as-we-cannot, as-we-cannot-be, as-we-cannot-be-there, as-we-do-not, as-we-do-not-think, as-we-do-not-think-there-is, as-we-do-not-think-there-is-anything, as-we-do-not-think-it-is, as-we-do-not-think-it-is-necessary

6. as-we-do-not-feel, as-we-found, as-we-are-not, as-we-wished, as-we-thought, as-we-did, as-we-did-not, as-we-did-not-know, as-we-had-not, as-we-had-not-been

---

7. as-we-have-been-there, as-we-know-there-is, as-we-know-there-is-not, as-we-think-there-is, as-we-think-there-is-not, as-we-think-there-is-nothing, as-we-introduced, as-we-had-been-there

8. as-we-trust, as-we-trusted, as-we-promised, as-we-brought, as-we-tried, as-we-bring, as-we-produce, as-we-provide, as-we-crossed, as-we-appreciate, as-we-drove

9. as-well(-will), as-well-as, as-well-as-possible, as-well-as-can-be, as-well-as-usual, as-will-be-seen, as-will-be-known, as-will-be-said, as-will-become

10. as-soon-as, as-soon-as-possible, as-soon-as-we, as-soon-as-we-can, as-soon-as-we-know, as-soon-as-we-know-there-is, as-soon-as-we-are

11. as-satisfactory, as-satisfactory-as, as-satisfactorily, as-certain, as-certain-as, as-said, as-suggested, as-such, as-soon-as-he, as-soon-as-he-is(-has)

12. as-soon-as-that, as-soon-as-that-is(-has), as-soon-as-it-is(-has), as-soon-as-it-is-possible, as-soon-as-it-can-be, as-soon-as-they, as-soon-as-they-have, as-soon-as-they-have-been, as-soon-as-they-were

---

13. this-is(-has), this-has-been, this-is(-has)-not, this-has-not-been, this-is(-has)-done, it-is-his(-as), as-has-been, there-is-some, there-is-something

14. it-is-certain, it-is-certain-that, it-is(-has)-certainly, it-is(-has)-certainly-not, it-has-certainly-not-been, it-has-certainly-been, for-his-sake

15. it-is-satisfactory, it-is-satisfactory-that, it-is-said, as-is-usual, as-is-known, as-is-now, is-satisfactory, it-is-simple, it-is-simply

16. it-is-suggested, it-is-seen, it-is-seen-that, as-is(-has), as-is(-has)-the, as-is-the-case, is-as(-his), this-city, in-this-city

17. in-these-cities, this subject, on-this-subject, on-these-subjects, in-these-subjects, in-all-these-subjects, this-side, on-this-side, on-these-sides

18. this-section, in-this-section, in-these-sections, in-all-these-sections, these-sentences, in-these-sentences, this-site, these-sites

## PRACTICE MATERIAL 4

(a) *Property*

As-we-can-see from here, building has-been started[10] on-this-side-of-the High-Road. As-soon-as[20]-we-know-there-is a house available, we-shall make[30] an offer for-it, as-we-wish to-live in[40]-this area. The agent states-that all-the houses on[50]-this-side-of-the road have already-been sold, but[60]-that this-is-not-the case on-the-other-side.[70] We-have asked-him to-reserve a house for-us[80] in-this-section of-the road, as-we-do-not[90]-wish to-be a long-way from-the shops and[100]-the station,

since-we-have-no car. The houses are[110]-not expensive, and it-is-certain-
that we-can sell[120] our present house at a fair price. As-promised, we[130]-
are writing to Mr-Smith as-soon-as-possible on[140]-this-subject to-tell-
him when our-own house will[150]-be up for-sale.                    (154)


## (b) *Annual report*

The figures now before-you are as-satisfactory as-the[10] figures for-last-
year. This-has-been achieved in-spite[20]-of rising costs, and it-is-certain
that-these results[30] would-not-have-been possible in-the-circumstances
unless every[40] member-of our staff had worked as-well-as-possible.[50]

As-will-be-seen, the report-contains little information about[60]-the
new plant, as-we-shall-not-be in-a[70]-position to assess-the value of-this-
section until it[80]-has-been in operation for-some-months. It-is-certain,[90]
however, that-this-section of-our factory is-as busy[100] as-we-thought it-
would-be, and-this-is a[110] source of-satisfaction to-us. Whilst on-this-
subject, I[120]-must tell-you that, if-the new plant is-satisfactory,[130] we-
shall build a similar one as-soon-as-possible,[140] as-we-think-that-the
present is-as good a[150] time for development as-we-are likely-to-have
for[160]-a-long-time.

It-is-suggested that-the dividend shall[170]-be one per-cent higher-than
last-year. This-is[180] proposed as-we-have-done well during-the past-
year,[190] and as-we-expect to-do as-well or even[200] better during-the
current-year.                                                       (205)


## (c) *Parliamentary speech*

The Right-Honourable-Gentleman-concluded: "It-is-satisfactory for-
us[10] to-be-able-to-state that-we-are doing as[20]-well-as-can-be expected
in-the-present circumstances. Trade[30] in-this-section has-not-been as
steady as-is[40]-usual, but-this-is-not a matter that-we-can[50]-control. It-
is-certain-that we-have taken advantage of[60] all-such export opportunities as-we-have-had.

"We-do[70]-not expect-the recession to continue, as-we-trust that[80]-
conditions will soon be as-satisfactory as-before. As-we[90]-do-not-think-
there-is any-further cause for alarm,[100] this-is to-be-the last statement
from this-side[110]-of-the House on-this-subject."                  (116)


## (d) *Letter from auctioneer*

Dear-Sir, As-we-promised that-we-would give-you[10]-the chance to
see-the new items as-soon-as[20]-possible, we-are-sending-you-the list at-
once. As[30]-we-do-not-wish to-sell-the goods in-these[40]-sections at-a-

loss, and as-we-feel you-are[50] almost-certainly able-to-make a reasonable bid, we-shall[60] do as-much-as we-can to help-you.

As[70]-we-know-that other-people as-well-as yourself are[80] interested in-these-subjects, it-is-suggested that-you attend[90]-the auction in-person. As-we-cannot take-steps to[100] hold-up-the bidding, we-are certain-that you-will[110] arrive as-soon-as-it-is-possible. Yours-faithfully, (119)

### (e) *Report on proposed extension*

As-will-be-seen from this-sketch of-the proposed[10] extension, it-is-certain to-be of-great-advantage to[20]-us, as-we-shall-be-able-to store more stock[30] in-there as-soon-as-it-is finished. In-these[40]-circumstances, as-we-produce more-and-more goods, it-is[50]-simply a question of-transferring them from-the old premises[60] in-this-city.

As-well-as-the extra space shown[70] in-this-sketch, it-is-satisfactory to say-that those[80]-sections of-the old premises that-we-do-not-need[90] will-not-be left empty, as-we-can let them.[100] The rent offered is-as satisfactory as-we-are likely[110] to-receive in-the-circumstances, and it-is-suggested that[120]-we sign-the lease as-soon-as-possible. (128)

## SELECTED PHRASES 5

1. last-year, last-few, last-few-years, for-last-year, during-the-last-year, last-few-days, last-few-months, at-last, at-least
2. just-in-time, just-now, just-after, just-enough, fast-as, as-fast-as, just-as, against-us
3. first-of-all, first-time, for-the-first-time, first-thing, first-things, first-hand, first-hand-information, first-hand-knowledge
4. first-class, first-class-quality, first-instance, in-the-first-instance, first-information, first-cost, first-costs, at-first-cost
5. at-first, at-first-hand, at-first-appearance, at-first-appearances, for-the-first, in-the-first, in-the-first-case, first-place, in-the-first-place, very-first
6. Sunday-next, Monday-next, Tuesday-next, Wednesday-next, Thursday-next, Friday-next, Saturday-next

## PRACTICE MATERIAL 5

### (a) *Report on a business*

At-last I-am-able-to give-you first-hand[10]-information regarding-the first-class organisation in-which-you-are[20]-interested. At-first-appear-ance, the results of-the last-few[30]-years do-not seem-to-be as-good-as might[40] be hoped, but further investigation shows that-the business has[50] progressed as-fast-as could-be expected and-is just[60]-now in a very-satisfactory position. The figures for-last[70]-year show that for-the-first-time this-company has[80] made a large profit, and-the-results are at-least[90] as-satisfactory as-those for-any similar-company.

I-suggest[100] that-the first-thing for-you to-do is-to[110] call in and see-me at-my office on-Monday[120]-next, when I-can show you at-first-hand some[130] trading figures for-the-last-few-years. (137)


## (b) *Letter to stamp dealer*

Dear-Sirs, I-am interested just-now in buying some[10] stamps in first-class-condition, and-I-shall-be-pleased[20] if-you-will in-the-first-instance let-me-have[30] your price-list. I-wish to-have this list by[40] Friday-next, and-I-shall-be interested to know whether[50] you have any first-day-covers available just-now.

I[60]-am working as-fast-as I-can to-set-up[70] a new business in-this-town. It-is-important that[80]-the stamps shall-be of first-quality only, as first[90]-appearances are of-great importance in-such-cases. During-the-last[100]-few-days, I-have-been to-several dealers but[110] have-not found anything that-is quite suitable. Yours-faithfully,[120] (120)


## SELECTED PHRASES 6

1. to-appear, it-appears, it-appears-that, it-appears-to-me, it-appeared, it-appeared-that, it-appeared-to-me, will-appear, it-will-appear, it-will-appear-that
2. he-appears, he-appeared, when-he-appears, when-he-appeared, have-appeared, in-which-it-appears, they-appear, they-appeared, it-would-appear
3. per-month, per-minute, per-term, per-cent, per-annum, per-head, as-per, per-day, per-kilogramme
4. Hyde-Park, Central-Park, Finsbury-Park, Elm-Park, Green-Park, Gidea-Park
5. car-park, local-park, local-parks, local-parks-committee, public-park, private-park
6. to-take-part, major-part, in-all-parts, in-all-parts-of-the-country, part-and-parcel, for-the-most-part, great-part(of), great-part(of)-the, part-of, part-of-the

---

7. all-parts-of-the-world, various-parts, various-parts-of-the-country, various-parts-of-the-world, your-part, my-part, for-your-part, for-my-part

8. several-parts, in-many-parts, to-part-with, to-part-with-the, on-your-part, on-my-part, large-part(of), greater-part(of), very-important-part

9. they-are, they-are-not, that-they-are, that-they-are-not, I-know-that-they-are, I-know-that-they-are-not, if-they-are, if-they-are-not, I-think-they-are, I-think-they-are-not, we-think-they-are, we-think-they-are-not

10. in-our, in-our-country, in-our-opinion, it-is-in-our-interests, in-our-view, in-our-interests, in-our-conditions, in-our-circumstances, in-our-society, in-our-bank

11. in-order, in-order-that, in-order-that-they-are, in-order-that-we-may, in-order-to, in-order-to-have, in-order-to-be-sure

12. to-assure, to-assure-the, to-assure-you, I-assure-you, I-can-assure-you, we-can-assure-you, you-can-be-assured, you-may-rest-assured, if-you-can-assure-us, we-are-assured, it-is-assured, they-assure-us

---

13. how-far, so-far, very-far, by-far-the-most, by-far-the-most-important, is-it-far, how-far-is-it, too-far, too-far-away, very-far-away

14. set-forth, so-forth, to-set-forth, we-set-forth, put-forth, I-put-forth, we-put-forth, purchase-agreement, it-is-agreed

15. Professor-Martin, Professor-Williams, Professor-of-Music, Professor-of-Geography, Anatomy-Professor, Regius-Professor, French-Professor, Chemistry-Professor

16. Colonel-Jones, Colonel-Jackson, Colonel-Thomas, Colonel-Cassels, Lieut-Col-Dean, Lieut-Col-Ball, Lieut-Col-Taylor, Lieut-Col-Riley

17. corporation-tax, corporation-law, transatlantic-corporations, Steel-Corporation, finance-corporations, overseas-corporations, American-corporations, aircraft-corporation

18. Superintendent-of-Police, Superintendent-Smith, Superintendent-Diamond, Superintendent-Chester, Police-Superintendent, Chief-Superintendent, parks-superintendent, works-superintendent

## PRACTICE MATERIAL 6

(a) *Notice to staff*

It-is-in-our-interests that all-members of-the[10] staff attend-the course of-lectures to-be given during[20]-the-next-few-weeks in-various-parts of-this-town.[30] It-appears from-the programmes that-the charge will-be[40] £1 per-head. In-order-to-be-sure of[50] a place at-all-the lectures, tickets will-have to[60]-be bought very-far in-advance. The speakers include Professor[70]-James, who-is-the Professor-of-Law at-the Central[80]-Park Institute, and-Colonel-Thompson, who-is-the Latin-Professor[90] at-the Elm-Park College. In-order-that-there shall[100]-be as-much variety as-possible, there-will-also-be[110] representatives of-several overseas-corporations present to-take-part in[120]-the general discussion.

We-have studied-the subjects on-which[130]-the speakers are to-lecture, as set-forth in-the[140] programmes, and-we-can-assure-you that-they-are by[150]-far-the-most instructive talks to-be given here.(159)

### (b) *Letter from publisher*

Dear Superintendent-Hall, In-our-opinion, a book dealing-with[10] your duties in-all-parts-of-the-world would-be[20] of-great-interest. We-can-assure-you that-it-appears[30] to-us that a book of-this-kind would find[40] readers in-various-parts-of-the-country, if-not many[50]-parts-of-the-world.

I-can-say-that for-my[60]-part you-may-rest-assured you have my support, but,[70] in-order-to-be-sure that-the-directors of-this[80]-corporation agree to-the project, it-is-necessary for-us[90] to-have more details. Perhaps you-would let-us-know[100] to-which parts-of-the-world you have-been and[110] how-far your duties enabled-you to-travel to-different-parts[120]-of-the-countries you visited.

In-order-that-we[130]-may assess-the length of-the book, may-we-know[140] if-you have any photographs to include ? It-may-be[150] that-you would-not want to-part-with personal photographs.[160] It-would-appear that-there-is-some possibility that-we[170]-could supply general views of-certain-parts—and, if-they[180]-are available, we-shall use them—but-there-are other[190]-parts on-which we-have-no material at-all.

As[200]-soon-as-we-have a decision from-the-corporation, we[210]-shall at-once let-you-know. Yours-truly,                    (218)

### (c) *Report on overseas visit*

During-the course of-the past-year, some members of[10]-this-corporation went to-many-parts-of-the-world in[20]-order-that-they-might find out something about-the methods[30] being used in different-parts-of-the-countries they visited.[40] They-assure-us that by-far-the-most advanced of[50]-these-countries is very-far behind as-compared-with-the[60] progress we-have made in-our-own procedures in-our[70]-bank. In-order-that-you-may-be aware of-the[80] detailed findings, Colonel-Wilson (who led-the team) is-to[90] make-out a report in-which-the results are fully[100] set-forth.

In-some-parts, our men were able-to[110]-go to-the game-parks. They-did-not have to[120]-go very-far out-of town to-reach them. In[130]-fact, they-were easier to-get to than-the local[140]-parks in-our-own-country. It-appears-that they used[150] about four films per-day, and-it-is-agreed that[160] some-time be set-aside to show them.                    (168)

## (d) *Parliamentary statement on working conditions*

The Secretary-of-State has set-forth the figures per[10]-month and-the figures per-annum. It-appears-that for[20]-the-most-part he-is too-far-away to-assure[30] himself of-the position, and-for-the greater-part-of[40]-the time he-must-be-assured by others. In-this[50] part-of his report, however, we-are-assured that-the[60] total hours shown per-head and per-day are accurate.[70]

Speaking at-the Central-Park Hall, the Secretary-of-State[80] said-that it-appeared-to-him that a great-part[90] of-each day was wasted. It-was, however, in-our[100]-own-interests to-assure-the labour force adequate rest periods.[110] Research carried-out by Professor-Rennie and Professor-Young for[120]-some overseas-corporations showed that some-part-of-the trouble[130] was fatigue. Continuing, he-said: "These eminent psychology-professors tell[140]-us-that half-an-hour spent visiting a local-park[150] would-be very-far from a waste-of-time in[160]-terms-of-production per-minute. How-far-the suggestion put[170]-forth in-the report sent by-the doctors will help[180] in-our-circumstances we-cannot-be-sure, but it-is[190]-agreed that-it-should-be tried."                    (196)

## SELECTED PHRASES 7

1. at-all, at-all-costs, at-all-events, at-all-times, by-all, by-all-means, by-all-accounts, by-all-reports, by-all-agreements, by-all-men
2. if-only, if-only-it-is(-has), if-only-it-is(-has)-not, it-is(-has)-only, that-it-is(-has)-only, that-it-has-only-been, only-just, it-is(-has)-only-just, that-it-is(-has)-only-just, he-can-only, he-can-only-be
3. we-can-only-be, I-have-only, I-have-only-been, I-have-only-just, I-have-only-just-been, I-may-only, they-may-only, they-may-only-have
4. it-will-only, it-will-only-be, it-will-only-be-there, I-will-only-say, they-will-only-say, they-will-only-sign, they-will-only-take
5. fellow-members, fellow-directors, to-make-application, formal-application, in-all, in-all-this, for-all, for-all-the
6. only-been, only-been-there, we-are-only, you-are-only, who-are-only, not-only, it-is-not-only, we-have-not-only

## PRACTICE MATERIAL 7

### (a) *Report*

We-have-only-just-received your-letter asking-us to[10] obtain for-you at-all-costs the information that-you[20] and your fellow-directors need. We-shall by-all-means[30] do what we-can, but by-all-accounts it-is[40]-only-the few to-whom first-hand-information will-be[50] given.

We-have-only-just-been able-to-make-the[60] first-contact, and-we-can-only-say at-present that[70] all-parts-of-the-country are officially closed to-the[80]-press. It-may-only-be for-a-few-days, or[90] it-may-be for-several-weeks. We-can-assure-you[100] that news of any importance is at-all-costs being[110] kept secret.

We-are-only able-to say-that we[120]-shall do everything we-can to help-you by-all[130]-means in-our-power and-with-the assistance of fellow[140]-members of-the-profession. However, we-can-only-do very[150]-little. (151)

## (b) *Report (continued)*

It-has-only-been two weeks since-this-matter was[10]-made public, and-we-have at-all-times been-contacted[20] first-hand by-all-men working with-us. By-all[30]-reports, nothing at-all definite has-been-said.

At-all[40]-events, it-would-not do any harm to-make-application[50] to-the Secretary-of-State. He-may-only-have-the[60] same information as-we-have, or he-may know if[70]-it-is only-just a matter-of-time. By-all[80]-means take any action you wish, but-we-can-only[90]-hope that-you-will keep-us informed at-all-times,[100] as-we-wish at-all-costs to-avoid covering the[110] same ground. (112)

## SELECTED PHRASES 8

1. had-been, I-have-been, I-had-been, we-have-been, we-had-been, they-had-been, can-only-have-been, already-been

2. recently-been, only-been, certainly-been, he-has-recently-been, it-has-recently-been, previously-been, may-have-been, never-been, obviously-been

3. has-not-been, had-not-been, I-had-not-been, we-had-not-been, it-has-been, it-has-not-been, he-has-been, he-has-not-been, this-has-been, this-has-not-been

4. she-has-been, it-has-only-been, I-have-not-been, we-have-not-been, has-been, if-he-has-not-been, if-it-has-not-been, as-has-been, what-has-been

5. rather-than, larger-than, smaller-than, quicker-than, higher-than, nearer-than, shorter-than, sooner-than, richer-than

6. farther-than, harder-than, better-than, greater-than, fewer-than, more-than, bigger-than, longer-than, much-more-than

7. later-on, carry-on, to-carry-on, carried-on, carrying-on, earlier-on, further-on, farther-on

8. he-carried-on, going-on, I-am-going-on, I-carried-on, I-carry-on, what-is-going-on
9. I-have-been-there, recently-been-there, more-than-their, to-carry-on-their, carried-on-their, has-not-been-there, had-not-been-there, he-has-been-there
10. only-been-there, greater-than-their, we-had-been-there, bigger-than-their, better-than-their, she-has-been-there, we-have-not-been-there
11. your-own, her-own, our-own, their-own, for-your-own, for-her-own, for-their-own, of-your-own, of-her-own, of-our-own, of-their-own
12. in-your-own, in-her-own, in-your-own-interests, in-her-own-interests, their-own-interests, to-your-own, to-her-own, to-our-own, to-their-own

---

13. my-own, my-own-way, my-own-case, in-my-own, in-my-own-interests, my-own-words
14. in-his-own, in-his-own-interests, of-his-own, to-his-own, for-his-own, in-their-own, in-our-own
15. I-am-not, you-will-not, they-will-not, this-will-not, this-will-not-be, it-will-not-be, he-will-not, he-will-not-be, I-do-not, I-did-not, we-do-not-know
16. is-it-not, certainly-not, it-is-(-has)-certainly-not, were-not, he-may-not, she-may-not, they-may-not, you-may-not, definitely-not, they-are-not
17. at-once, upon-us, depend-upon-us, Monday-next, Tuesday-next, Wednesday-next, Thursday-next, Friday-next, Saturday-next, Sunday-next
18. at-the-beginning, from-the-beginning, in-the-beginning, from-the-beginning-to-the-end, if-it-is-convenient, if-it-is-not-convenient, at-your-convenience, at-my-convenience, at-their-convenience.

## PRACTICE MATERIAL 8

(a) *Letter about North Sea gas*

Dear-Charles, We-have recently-been drilling in-the North[10] Sea on-our-own. The area, which-has-been worked[20] before, is richer-than we-expected in gas—and-larger[30]-than we-had-been led to-believe. The gas-field[40] is nearer-than we-thought it-would-be, so-the[50] land pipe can-be shorter-than the estimate. It-will[60]-therefore be laid sooner-than-the date given. This-has[70]-been a difficult job from-the-beginning, and-we-are[80] certainly-not going to-be-able-to carry-on-the[90] work without you for very-long. We-have asked some[100] experts to-come at-once, but-they-will-not-be[110] here until Thursday-next. They-are going to-carry-on[120] as-well-as they can on-their-own until you[130]-can reach here. It-is-certainly-not in-your-own[140]-interests to-waste time; and, if-it-is-convenient, I[150]-suggest you try to arrive at-all-costs by Wednesday[160]-next.

I-am-not at-all sure how-long it[170]-will-be before-the other-companies send in-their-own[180] men to inspect-the site. You-may depend-upon-us[190] to-deal-with-the-matter. They-have-had more-than[200]-their share of-luck; and-they-are-not too-pleased[210] that-it-is our-own turn now. A release to[220]-the-press has already-been made, and-I-shall call[230] a conference later-on. My-own view is-that it[240]-should definitely-not-be set too-far ahead, for if[250]-it-is you-may-not-be-able-to be there.[260] Yours,                                                   (261)

## (b) *Letter to prospective employee*

Dear-Miss-Syms, I-interviewed you earlier-on this-week.[10] I-told-you at-the-beginning that-this-will-not[20]-be an easy post, as-you-will-be carrying-on[30] the work-of someone else. She dealt-with things in[40]-her-own way, and your-own ideas may-be different.[50] The office may-be larger-than you thought it-would[60]-be, and you-may-not-be-able-to find a[70] room smaller-than that for-some-time. You-will-not[80] in-any-event be expected to change anything at-first.[90]

As-far-as-the salary is concerned, we-had previously[100]-been paying lower-than our scale rates, as-we-had[110] to-employ agency staff for-a-time. In-your-own[120] case, we-are-prepared to pay more-than would-be[130] usual, because-of-the special difficulties, and you-may depend[140]-upon-us to-review this regularly.

You-should-have already[150]-been given full-particulars of-the club activities. These have[160] recently-been extended to include a drama-association. The chess[170] group has only-been formed in-the-last-week.

I[180]-look-forward to seeing-you on-Monday-next. Yours-truly, (190)

## (c) *Company report on redundancy*

It-has always-been our policy to-take action at[10]-once, rather-than to-leave matters to-take-their-course.[20] This-has-not-been an easy time for-this-corporation,[30] as profits have-been lower-than usual, while costs are[40] already higher-than last-year. It-is definitely-not to[50]-be expected that our-own results will-be any better[60]-than those of any-other-company, and it-will-not[70]-be a surprise to-you to-hear that-the trouble[80] started at-the-beginning of-the-year.

For-my-part,[90] it-has-certainly been a difficult decision to-make men[100] redundant, but-they-are-not unaware of what-has-been[110] happening. It-is-in-their-own best-interests to-find[120] other work at-once. They-may depend-upon-us to[130]-do as-much-as we-can to-suit their-convenience.[140] To-carry-on-their jobs here will-not-be of[150] help to anyone, and-they-have already-been told so.[160]

My-own feeling is-that we should-have another meeting[170] as-soon-as-possible—at-all-costs by Friday-next,[180] and-even earlier-than that if-it-is-convenient to[190]-do-so. (192)

(d) *Letter to student*

Dear Mr-Smith, The latest report has recently-been sent[10] to-your employers. For-your-own sake, and-in-your[20]-own-interests, you-should work harder-than you have-been[30] doing during-the-last-few-months. Your tutors have-been[40] at pains to-impress upon-us that-you could do[50] much better-than you have-been doing so-far. The[60] amount of-your-own time devoted to study should-be[70] greater-than it-has-been. It-would-be to-your[80]-own advantage if-you made your hours of-leisure shorter[90]-than they-have-been and-if-you arrived at college[100] earlier-than is usual. If-you do-not take-steps[110] at-once, you-will-be very-sorry later-on; you[120]-will-not like it when-you find that others have[130]-been given jobs much better-than your-own.

You-will[140] hear on-Monday-next when-it-is-convenient for-you[150] to see-the Principal. He-is-not anxious to-delay[160]-the meeting, any-more-than you-are, and-I-have[170]-been informed that-it-is-likely to-be at-the[180]-beginning of next session. Yours-truly, (186)

## SELECTED PHRASES 9

1. which-have, which-have-not, which-have-been, which-have-not-been, who-have, who-have-not, who-have-been, who-have-not-been, I-have, as-we-have, can-only-have
2. those-who-have, those-who-have-not, those-who-have-been, those-who-have-not-been, those-who-have-had, those-who-have-not-had, those-who-have-done, those-who-have-not-done, ought-to-have, ought-to-have-been, ought-to-have-had, ought-to-have-done
3. group-of, capable-of, plenty-of, state-of-affairs, part-of, exchange-of, range-of, set-of, set-of-the, state-of, state-of-the, state-of-things
4. out-of, out-of-the, out-of-touch, copy-of, copy-of-the, plenty-of-the, sort-of, in-spite-of, in-spite-of-the, instead-of, instead-of-the
5. part-of-the, present-state-of, present-state-of-things, report-of, shortage-of, present-state-of-affairs, rate-of-interest, rate-of-exchange, rate-of-pay, rate-of-tax

6. rate-of-taxation, rate-of-income-tax, set-of-things, set-of-books, set-of-requirements, out-of-doors, age-of, page-of, number-of, large-number-of, great-number-of

---

7. set-off, paid-off, wipe-off, to-make-off, better-off, to-take-off, I-set-off, make-off, take-off, to-wipe-off-the, to-take-off-the
8. which-of-their, range-of-their, out-of-their, set-of-their, group-of-their, copy-of-their, paid-off-their, to-wipe-off-their, to-take-off-their
9. Monday-afternoon, Tuesday-afternoon, Wednesday-afternoon, Thursday-afternoon, Friday-afternoon, Saturday-afternoon, Sunday-afternoon, yesterday-afternoon
10. Monday-evening, Tuesday-evening, Wednesday-evening, Thursday-evening, Friday-evening, Saturday-evening, Sunday-evening, yesterday-evening
11. this-afternoon, those-afternoons, these-afternoons, tomorrow-afternoon, this-evening, those-evenings, these-evenings, tomorrow-evening
12. at-all-events, such-events, which-events, in-the-event(of), this-event, course-of-events, in-effect, to-effect, this-effect, into-effect

## PRACTICE MATERIAL 9

(a) *Letter to British Rail*

Dear-Sirs, We-thank-you for sending-us a copy[10]-of-the new railway-timetable and-for-the set-of[20] leaflets. It-appears-that-you-will-be making-the sort[30]-of changes that-will affect our-own times, and-we[40]-shall-be-glad if-you-will send-us a set[50]-of application-forms. We-think-that-the number-of cheaper[60] fares for parties has-been reduced, and-we-shall-be[70]-glad if, when sending-the set-of-forms for-us[80] to-make-application for group rates, you-will-say whether[90] this-state-of-affairs is-to-continue. If-it-is[100] to-be part-of your future policy, we-can-only-suggest[110] that-we-send a senior official to-meet you.[120] If-you prefer, you could call-upon-us; and, in[130]-that event, an appointment on-Thursday-afternoon would-be-convenient[140] for-us and would give-you plenty-of time to[150]-send a reply to-us by early next-week. Yours[160]-faithfully,                                              (161)

(b) *Newsletter*

The set-of proofs of-the report-of-the chairman's[10]-speech at-the meeting held on-Friday-evening shows that,[20] in-spite-of-the adverse-conditions which-have recently-been[30] met in-all-parts-of-the-world, we-can at[40]-all-events be-pleased with-the-present-state-of our[50] accounts. The effect-of-the present-state-of-affairs has[60]-been small as-compared-with what-was expected, and-we[70]-hope that-this-state-of-things will enable-us to[80]-carry-on.

An inspection of-the first page-of-the[90] proofs will make-clear what-is-the position in-our[100] group-of-companies abroad. It-will-be-seen-that Colonel[110]-Wilson and-the Works-Superintendent, who-have-been on a[120] tour of-our-corporations, returned on-Monday-afternoon. Those-who[130]-have-had-the opportunity of-hearing what sort-of progress[140] has-been possible, in-spite-of-conditions which-have-not[150] always-been very-good, have said-that-we ought-to[160]-have a special meeting. It-is-agreed that-these two[170] gentlemen will come to-discuss-the-matter tomorrow-afternoon. It[180]-must-be realized from-the-beginning that-the-meeting is[190] being held in-the-interests of all-those-who-have[200]-not-had-the opportunity to-hear-the first-hand account[210] of-the tour. (213)

(c) *Details of conference*

The programme of-the-conference that starts on-Monday-next[10] has-been-arranged particularly for-those who-have-become out[20]-of-touch with-the present-state-of-things in-the[30]-profession.

Delegates will-be received on-Monday-afternoon, and-they[40]-will-have a few hours in-which-their general-arrangements[50] should-be-made. The same evening, the report-of-the[60] President will-be given. A cold supper will-be served[70] out-of-doors. On Tuesday-morning, there-are a number[80]-of talks on a wide range-of subjects. On Tuesday[90]-afternoon, several distinguished-professors will each speak to a different[100] group-of delegates. On Tuesday-evening, instead-of a set[110]-of reports, there-will-be-the only-completely free evening[120] out-of-the whole week.

The set-of reports will[130]-be presented on-Wednesday-morning, and-there-will-be plenty[140]-of time for questions. The matter of-the rate-of[150]-pay and-the shortage-of new and-fully-qualified members[160] will-also-be discussed whenever-convenient during-the morning. Wednesday[170]-afternoon will-be a particular pleasure to-those-who-have[180] an interest in games out-of-doors, and a great[190]-number-of activities have-been planned. On-Wednesday-evening, a[200] Professor-of-Music is-to give a recital together-with[210] a short talk. Those-who-have-not-been issued with[220] tickets will-not-be admitted.

Any members who-have-not[230] received a copy-of-the programme should make-application at[240]-their-own-convenience, but at-all-events by Friday-next,[250] to-this office. (253)

(d) *Chairman's report*

Ladies-and-Gentlemen, It-is-certainly a pleasure this-afternoon[10] to put before-you such satisfactory-results, which-have-been[20] much better-than we-thought possible a year-ago. In[30]-spite-of all-the difficulties which-have-had to-be[40] faced during-the part-of-the year under-con-sideration, your[50]-corporation is able-to-report a small-profit instead-of[60]-the loss which-was feared.

By-far-the-most-important[70]-contribution has-been-made by-all those-who-have-done[80]-their very-best at-all-times. Out-of-their work[90] has come success. Not-only has-this-corporation made a[100] profit for-the-first-time, but it-has-been possible[110] also to-wipe-off a total-of £150,000[120] in corporation-tax, which-has built up[130] over-several-years. There-has-been a rise in-the[140] rate-of-taxation, but-we-hope to-set-off-the[150] expected increase by economies in-various-parts of-the business.[160]

In-regard-to-the present-state-of trade, I-can[170]-tell-you that-there-are a number-of reasons for[180] thinking that an improvement is-not very-far-away. It[190]-appears-that-the state-of-the country's economy is improving,[200] too, in-spite-of-the instability in-the rate-of[210]-exchange for-the dollar. You-will-remember-that we-had[220] to postpone putting into-effect part-of our plans for[230] extending-the plant. It-is-satisfactory to-be-able-to[240]-report that-the second phase can now be put into[250]-effect at-once.

You-may-rest-assured that your-directors[260]-continue-to-watch all-such-events at-home-and-abroad[270] and in-the European markets as may affect any part[280]-of this-corporation's business.          (284)

## SELECTED PHRASES 10

1. Pacific-Ocean, Atlantic-Ocean, North-Atlantic-Ocean, South-Atlantic-Ocean, Arctic-Ocean, Antarctic-Ocean, Indian-Ocean

2. for-your-information, for-their-information, for-her-information, further-information, for-his-information, this-information, any-information, recent-information

3. Football-Association, Library-Association, First-Aid-Association, Swimming-Association, Trade-Association, British-Medical-Association, your-association, Traders'-Association, Geographical-Association

4. occasion, on-such-occasions, on-this occasion, on-these-occasions, section, in-this-section, in-these-sections, in-some-sections, in-which-section

5. in-connection-with, your-connections, trade-connections, trade-conditions, world-conditions, in-these-conditions, in-any-conditions

6. in-possession, in-(a)-position, we-are-in-(a)-position, in-this-position, in-succession, no-decision, trade-recession, no-justification

## PRACTICE MATERIAL 10

(a) *Associations*

Groups of-people who-are-interested in-the-same sort[10]-of things often form themselves into an association, if-they[20]-are in-a-position to-do-so.

In-this-connection,[30] and-for-your-information, we-enclose a list of-some[40] of-the best-known associations. Some are professional-associations, such[50]-as-the British-Medical-Association, the Architectural-Association and-the[60] Bankers'-Association. Others are-concerned with particular subjects, such-as[70]-the Geographical-Association, the Gliding-Association, the Historical-Association and[80]-the Travel-Association. Various others such-as-the Veterinary-Association,[90] the Auditors'-Association, the Press-Association, the Employers'-Associations and[100]-the Research-Associations play an important-part in-our daily[110]-lives.

Such associations may-have branches on-the-other-side[120]-of-the Atlantic-Ocean as-well, and-the branches may[130]-be divided into sections. (134)

(b) *Letter to association secretary*

Dear-Miss-Thomas, We-are-very-pleased to-have-the[10] pamphlets dealing-with-the Pacific-Ocean. We-think-these will[20]-be of-great-interest to a number-of members of[30]-our-society.

We-wonder if-there-is-any chance of[40]-your-association producing further-information about-the South-Atlantic-Ocean.[50] We-have-only-just found a book on-the-subject,[60] and-we-enclose a copy-of it for-your-information.[70] It-is-worth giving special-attention to-those-sections that[80] deal-with-the seasons of-the-year. In-those-sections,[90] as you-will-see, recent-information has-been included from[100]-the various weather-associations regarding-conditions to-be expected in[110]-the oceans of-the-world at different seasons of-the[120]-year. Yours-truly, (123)

## SELECTED PHRASES 11

1. if-it, if-it-is(-has), if-it-is(-has)-not, if-it-was, if-it-was-not, if-it-were, if-it-were-not, in-which-it-is(-has), in-which-it-is(-has)-not, in-which-it-has-been, in-which-it-says

2. I-think-it-is(-has), I-think-it-is(-has)-not, I-think-it-is-necessary, depend-upon-it, from-it, for-it, for-it-is(-has), for-it-is(-has)-not, by-it, by-its(-itself), by-its-means

3. able-to, able-to-make, able-to-make-arrangements, I-am-able-to, they-were-able-to, we-were-able-to, if-we-are-able-to-make, be-able-to, to-be-able-to, I-shall-be-able-to

4. unable-to, unable-to-make, I-am-unable-to, I-am-unable-to-find, we-are-unable-to, we-are-unable-to-control, they-were-unable-to

5. for-my-part, all-parts, all-parts-of-the-world, other-parts, in-all-parts-of-the-country, various-parts, part-and-parcel, great-part(of), great-number-of, large-part(of)-the, large-number-of-the

6. board-of-directors, board-and-lodging, Electricity-Board, your-board, Water-Board, on-board, Airways-Board, British-Railways-Board, Gas-Board

---

7. I-will-not, I-will-not-be, I-am-not, I-am-not-in-a-position, I-do-not, I-do-not-know, I-do-not-think, I-do-not-think-it-is, I-do-not-think-it-is-necessary, I-do-not-think-there-is, you-will-not, you-will-not-be

8. you-are-not, they-are-not, we-will-not-be, we-will-not-be-there, we-will-not-say, we-will-not-consider-the-matter, they-did(-do)-not, they-did(-do)-not-know-that, certainly-not, it-is(-has)-certainly-not, this-will-not

9. have-not, are-not, was-not, we-are-not, I-would-not, I-would-not-be-there, we-would-not-be-there, they-would-not-be-there, this-would-not-be-the, they-would-not-consider-the-matter

10. don't, didn't, shan't, won't, aren't, can't, haven't, isn't, wasn't, weren't, wouldn't

11. sort-of, in-spite-of, in-spite-of-the, instead-of, instead-of-the, part-of, part-of-the, in-support-of, in-support-of-the, report-of-the

12. set-out, to-set-out, we-set-out, they-set-out, carried-out, I-carried-out, if-you-carried-out, brought-out, I-brought-out, we-brought-out

---

13. to-state, this-state, this-statement, in-this-statement, recent-statement, in-their-statement, several-statements, present-state, present-state-of, present-state-of-things, present-state-of-affairs

14. short-time, short-time-ago, at-some-time, at-some-time-or-other, at-the-same-time, for-some-time, for-some-time-past, for-some-time-to-come, at-one-time

15. from-time-to-time, at-all-times, lunch-time, second-time, spare-time, modern-times, valuable-time, no-time, at-any-time, this-time

16. those-words, in-those-words, these-words, in-these-words, in-his-own-words, common-words, in-other-words, few-words, in-a-few-words, to-say-a-few-words

17. many-words, how-many-words, in-the-words, words-a-minute, I-would, I-would-be, I-would-be-there, we-would, we-would-be, we-would-be-there

18. they-would-not-be, this-would, if-it-would-be, that-would, it-would-not, he-would-not-be, it-would-not-be, they-would, he-would-not-consider-the-matter, we-would-certainly-not

## PRACTICE MATERIAL 11

(a) (i) *Memo from Hotel Manager to Booking Clerk*

I-have-just-received a letter from Colonel-Dixon in[10]-connection-with a booking for full board-and-lodging. He[20]-cannot come at-the-time when-he-said he-would,[30] for-the reason set-out—that-is, that-he-will[40]-be in-other-parts-of-the-country for-the greater[50]-part-of-the time for-which he had booked. In[60]-the-circumstances, we-would usually require full payment; but, as[70]-he-is a most-important client of-the hotel, I[80]-do-not-think-it-is-necessary in-this-case. Instead[90]-of that, I-suggest that-we offer him different dates.[100] If-it-is-not-convenient for-us to-do-so,[110] let-me-know at-once, for-it would-be necessary[120] to-make other-arrangements. I-am-not sending-you a[130] copy-of his letter, as you-would get no-further[140]-information from-it than I-have-been able-to let[150]-you-have myself. If-you-carried-out a check first[160]-thing tomorrow-morning as-to-the present-state-of bookings,[170] you-would perhaps be-able-to let-me-have this[180]-information by lunch-time.　　　　　　　　　　　　　　　　　　　　　(184)

(ii) *Memo from Booking Clerk to Hotel Manager*

I-have-been unable-to-make-the change-of accommodation[10] set-out in-your memo of-yesterday. Instead-of that,[20] we-would-have-been able-to recommend Colonel-Dixon to[30] Mr-and-Mrs Graham, but they-would-not-consider-the[40]-matter at-all, as a large-number-of-the visitors[50] there take block bookings. It-is-only a short-time[60] before Colonel-Dixon is expected, and it-will-not-be[70] easy-to-find him a room. I-do-not-think[80]-there-is-any-doubt, however, that-we-shall be-able[90]-to-make-arrangements somewhere.　　　　　　　　　　　　　(94)

(iii) *Letter from Hotel Manager to client*

Dear Colonel-Dixon, Thank-you for-your-letter, setting out[10]-the reason-why you-are-unable-to take-up your[20] booking with-us. We-have-seen-the work that-has[30] recently-been brought-out under your name, and-we-are[40]-very-pleased that-you have-been asked-to-say a[50]-few-words to-the-members-of-the Historical-Association on[60]-the-subject of-your book. In-these-circumstances, we-will[70]-not-consider-the-matter of a cancellation fee.

We-are[80]-unable-to offer-you other accommodation ourselves, but-we-are[90] able-to-make-arrangements at-any-time for a room[100] in-another-part-of-the town, if-it-is-convenient[110] to-you to-take that.

As-requested, we-set-out[120] on a separate sheet the most recent-statements issued by[130]-the local-authority on-the present-state-of-affairs with[140]-regard-to archaeological sites in-this area. You-will-see[150]-that it-is-only a few-words, and you-may[160] wish to-go and see them yourself at-some-time[170] during your stay. Yours-truly,                    (175)


## (b) *Annual report*

The past-year has-been one in-which-it-has[10]-been difficult to-make-the progress that-was expected, as[20] set-out in-the report-of-the previous year. We[30]-have from-time-to-time carried-out large-contracts, but[40]-we-are-not-yet well-known, in-spite-of-the[50] efforts of-your-board at-all-times to-take advertising[60] space in-various-parts-of-the-country. There-will-not[70]-be any great-improvement in-the present-state-of-affairs[80] for-some-time-to-come, but I-do-not-think[90]-there-is-any-point in taking-up-the valuable-time[100] of-the-meeting, as-the position is fully set-out[110] in statements sent-out to-you a short-time-ago.[120]

I-would-like-to-say-a-few-words about-the[130] present-state-of our finances. We-have from-time-to[140]-time carried-out surveys, and-they-do-not show any[150] real cause for-the figures in-this-statement being as[160] bad as they-are. We-are-unable-to-control-the[170] situation; and, if-it does-not improve, we-shall-not[180]-be-able-to-continue with our plans for expansion. We[190]-would-certainly-not carry-out a large-number-of-the[200] projects we-had planned. It-is-satisfactory to-be-able[210]-to-state, however, that-the report-of-the-committee indicates[220] that-this-will-not affect-the recreation hall, which-has[230]-been proposed for-some-time-past. Your board-of-directors[240] hope-that a large-number-of-the staff will-be[250]-able-to take-part in-the activities provided.          (258)


## (c) *'Opinion' of counsel*

I-have spent much of-my valuable-time with-the[10]-directors of-your-company, and-I-cannot-say that-you[20]-will-be successful this-time in-your-action against the[30] local Electricity-Board. I-have-not seen-the most recent[40]-statements; but-there-were several-statements in-the-words of[50]-the witnesses themselves, which-would-be of-great-import-ance in[60]-support-of your claim. I-carried-out a survey on[70] various-parts-of-the land, and, if-it-was accurate[80] we should-be-able-to-make a better showing than[90] before. There-are a great-many-words of-evidence still[100] to-be read. I-do-not-wish, therefore, to arrange[110] a definite date for-the-meeting, in-case I-am[120]-unable-to keep it.          (124)

# SELECTED PHRASES 12

1. in-which-their, I-think-their, I-have-not-been-there, making-their, making-their-way, making-their-own-way

2. taking-their, taking-their-own, I-believe-there(-their), I-was-there, I-shall-be-there, I-shall-not-be-there, then-there-are-the, I-know-their(-there)

3. in-their(-there), in-their-opinion, in-their-view, in-their-interests, in-their-own-opinion

4. upon-their, depend-upon-their, had-been-there, she-will-be-there, they-will-be-there, they-will-not-be-there, he-will-not-be-there, let-us-be-there, if-you-can-be-there

5. in-which-there-is(-has), in-which-there-is(-has)-not, in-which-there-is-no, in-which-there-is-nothing, I-think-there-is(-has), I-think-there-is(-has)-not, I-think-there-is-no, I-think-there-is-nothing, although-there-is(-has), although-there-is(-has)-not, although-there-is-nothing

6. I-know-there-is(-has), I-know-there-is(-has)-not, I-know-there-is-nothing, I-am-sure-there-is, I-believe-there-is(-has), I-believe-there-is(-has)-not, I-believe-there-is-no, I-believe-there-is-nothing

---

7. some-other, at-some-other, some-other-way, some-other-ways, in-some-other-ways

8. some-other-cases, in-some-other-cases, some-other-means, by-some-other, by-some-other-means

9. in-some-other-respects, in-other-times, in-other-ways, in-other-directions

10. in-other-words, some-other-words, in-some-other-words, some-how-or-other, some-time-or-other

11. no-other, no-other-way, no-other-part, any-other, any-other-way, any-other-part, my-dear-friend, my-dear-Miss-Brown

12. he-may-have-been-there, only-been-there, we-had-been-there, greater-than-their, recently-been-there, more-than-their, finer-than-their, going-on-their

---

13. I-have-been-there, already-been-there, better-than-their, larger-than-their, higher-than-their, carry-on-their, to-carry-on-their, he-carried-on-their, I-carried-on-their

14. which-of(-have)-their, range-of-their, out-of-their(-there), group-of-their, copy-of-their, state-of-their, exchange-of-their, to-take-off-their, set-off-their, paid-off-their, to-wipe-off-their

15. for-there-is(-has), for-there-is(-has)-not, for-there-is-no-point, for-there-is-nothing, if-there-is(-has), if-there-is(-has)-not, if-there-were-not, if-there-is-anything, if-there-is-nothing

16. I-shall-therefore, we-shall-therefore, I-was-therefore, that-he-was-therefore, I-am-therefore, I-have-therefore, we-have-therefore, I-think-therefore, we-think-therefore

17. in-order, in-order-that-you-may, in-order-that-we-know, in-order-that-he-will, in-order-that-we-may

18. in-order-to, in-order-to-be, in-order-to-be-sure, in-order-to-have, in-order-to-avoid, in-order-to-take, in-order-to-take-advantage, in-order-to-take-part, in-order-to-put, in-order-to-put-forward

## PRACTICE MATERIAL 12

### (a) *Chairman's address*

Ladies-and-Gentlemen, I-think-there-is very-little that[10] I-can add on-the-subject of-the figures for[20]-the-year. Although-there-is much that-would-be better[30] said now, if-there-were-time, there-is-no-other[40]-way but to-call a special meeting. I-am-sure[50]-there-is some-other-means by-which we-can save[60]-the-company, other-than by becoming a very-small-part[70]-of a large overseas-corporation in-London. I-have-been[80] down-there to see-the board-of-directors, and-the[90] secretary of-the-company has also-been-there, in-order[100]-to make quite-sure we-are-not making a mistake.[110] In-fact, I-have recently-been-there again, in-order[120]-that-you-may-have-the offer in writing, and-I[130]-am-therefore sending-you a set-of-their accounts together[140]-with a copy-of-the chairman's speech. You-will-see[150]-that-the range-of-their interests is in-their-own[160]-opinion as wide as-it-can-be. However, when I[170]-was-there, I-felt that-they depend-upon-their well[180]-known lines too-much. Then-there-are some-other-cases[190] where I-believe-there-is much room for improvement. I[200]-know-there must-be points you-would wish to-raise.[210] I-shall-therefore now be-pleased to-answer questions, if[220]-there-is-anything that-you do-not understand. (228)

### (b) *Letter from information bureau*

Dear-Mrs Green, I-do-not-think-there-is a[10] consumers'-association in-your-own area. There-are some-others[20] near to-you, and-I-am-therefore sending-you-the[30] addresses, in-order-that-you-may take-advantage of-their[40] services. The new building in High-Street is bigger-than[50]-their old one, but for-my-part I-liked-the[60] old one better-than-their present one. They-were quite[70] unable-to carry-on-their work in-the old premises,[80] as-the rent alone was higher-than-their total income.[90] As-far-as-the High-Street premises are-concerned, I[100]-have recently-been-there; and, although-there-is more space[110] in-there, they-will-not-be-there for very-long[120] if-there-is some-other office available. I-shall-therefore[130] let-you-know at-once if-there-is-any change[140]-of address. Yours truly, (144)

(c) *Extract from lecture*

The speaker said: I-believe-there-is no-one who[10]-has-not at-least some interest in-this-subject. My[20]-dear-friend and colleague Professor-Waters says that many-people[30] are making-their-own-way somehow-or-other in-their[40] studies in-this-connection, and-I-am-sure-there-is[50] truth in-that. However, I-think-there-is a need[60] for talks of-this-kind, because I-know-there are[70] people who-have no-other-way of-finding-out-the[80] facts, for-there-are-no classes held in-their areas.[90]

The branches of-your-association have always done-their best[100] in-this-respect. They-have recently-been doing more-than[110]-their share in-order-to-be-sure that-those-who[120] live in towns in-which-there-is-no college could[130] take-part in-their-own classes. They-have set-off[140] expenses in-other-ways, and-I-hope-there-is no[150]-doubt that-they-will carry-on-their work for-some[160]-time-to-come.            (163)

(d) *Letter concerning property*

My-dear-Miss-Brown, In-reply-to-your-letter, I[10]-do-not-think-there-is any-other-way but to[20]-sell-the land to-this-corporation, if-you-can. They[30]-have offered to-send in a group-of-their men,[40] in-order-to take-advantage of-the whole range-of[50]-their resources. In-other-words, they-will-not make-up[60]-their minds until they can-be-sure that-it-is[70]-not-possible to obtain-the land by-some-other-means.[80] I-have-therefore agreed on-your behalf.

There-are some[90]-other-people who-are-interested in buying, and-their last[100] offer is much larger-than-their first one. In-some[110]-other-respects, however, they-are-not at-all suitable. Some[120]-of-them want to-meet you on-the estate next[130]-time they-are going-there to see-the land, if[140]-you-can-be-there too. I-am-sure-there-is[150] no harm in-it, and-I-shall-therefore make-the[160] necessary-arrangements. Yours-sincerely,            (164)

## SELECTED PHRASES 13

1. they-were, as-they-were, they-were-not, and-they-were-not, for-they-were-not, we-were, we-were-not, if-we-were
2. if-we-were-not, as-if-we-were, when-we-were, when-we-were-not, if-it-were, if-it-were-not, that-were
3. before-the-war, during-the-war, after-the-war, world-war, through-out-the-war, if-there-is-war
4. live-wire, telegraph-wires, several-wires, telephone-wire, telephone-wires, these-wires, Sir-James, yes-sir

5. per-annum, per-head, per-ton, per-day, per-pound, per-cent, it-would-appear, out-of-doors
6. let-us-know, to-let-us-know, please-let-us-know, let-us-have, to-let-us-have, please-let-us-have, this-letter, in-this-letter, these-letters, business-letters, for-sale

---

7. any-less-than, no-less-than, any-longer, any-longer-than, no-longer, no-longer-than, something-like, anything-else
8. where-else, somewhere-else, nowhere-else, everywhere-else, everywhere-else-in-the-world, I-would-like, we-would-like-to-say
9. this-week, these-weeks, next-week, last-week, previous-week, you-will, I-will-not, that-he-will, she-will-be, this-will, we-will
10. so-well, so-well-known, it-may-well-be, they-may-well-have, very-well, very-well-indeed, who-were, if-he-were, you-were, which-were-not, you-were-not
11. in-the-world, throughout-the-world, all-over-the-world, for-the-world, this-world, in-this-world, all-parts-of-the-world, various-parts-of-the-world
12. that-was, that-was-not, that-wasn't, this-was, this-was-not, this-wasn't, if-it-was, if-it-was-not, if-it-wasn't

---

13. several-weeks, past-few-weeks, next-few-weeks, in-a-few-weeks, as-well-as, as-well-as-possible, as-will(-well), as-will-be-seen, as-we-can, as-we-know
14. in-the-house, in-the-House-of-Commons, to-the-house, in-this-house, I-hope-that, I-hope-you-are-not, I-hope-there-is, I-hope-that-you-will, at-home, at-home-and-abroad, at-home-and-overseas
15. of-him, from-him, helped-him, tell-him, to-give-him, of-me, from-me, helped-me, tell-me, to-give-me
16. enable-himself, for-himself, by-himself, of-himself, helped-himself, enable-myself, for-myself, by-myself, of-myself, helped-myself
17. by-whom, for-whom, in-whom, to-whom, of-whom, with-whom, to-here(-hear), in-here, over-here
18. by-her, for-her, of-her, of-her-own, in-her, in-her-own, in-her-own-interests, by-herself

## PRACTICE MATERIAL 13

(a) *Letter from fashion house*

Dear Sir-John, We-thank-you for-your-enquiry, and[10]-we-have-pleasure in-sending-you-the list of-dates,[20] for-several-weeks ahead, of-the shows to-be held[30] by-this-House. Even if-you-cannot come next-week,[40] this-letter may still be used later-on instead-of[50] a ticket. If-you-were thinking of-coming later, it[60]-would-be as-well if-you-would please-let-us[70]-know as-soon-as-possible when-you plan to-visit[80]-us. I-hope-there-is at-least one date that[90]-is suitable.

We-are quite-sure that Lady Helen will[100] find something to-her taste in-our new collection. We[110]-would-like-to-say that-such a range-of items[120] can-be-found nowhere-else-in-the-world, not even[130] in Paris. Our special designer, Robert, who used to-be[140] responsible for Lady Helen's fittings, is-no-longer with-us.[150] He-was offered a large extra sum-of-money per[160]-annum to work in America, and-we-did-not-feel[170] we-had any right to ask-him to-stay over[180]-here. However, we-have-found a young lady who-appears[190] to-have a great-deal of-talent and-in-whom[200] we-have-the highest-confidence. We-hope-that-you-will[210]-be-pleased with-her work.

If-you-were to-let[220]-us-have a note of-your-requirements in-advance, we[230]-would make-sure that-we-had-the items in-the[240]-House by-the time of-your visit. Yours-sincerely,                    (249)

(b) *Statement on dividends*

You-will I-hope be-pleased with-the proposed dividend[10] of six per-cent. It-would-appear that, as-this[20]-is nothing-like-the figure that-was usual before-the[30]-war, some of-you think-that we-cannot-be doing[40] so-well. You-will, of-course, realize that-the value[50] of-money has changed very-much since-that-time. Also,[60] conditions of-trading throughout-the-world are no-longer what[70] they-were.

Some of-you have told-me that-you[80]-were thinking of-offering your shares for-sale. In-order[90]-to-avoid any-such-action on-your-part, since-it[100]-may-well-have an effect on-the-market both at[110]-home-and-overseas, I-would-like to-give-you-the[120] actual figures. This-will enable-you to compare-the results[130] before-the-war with-those during-the-war, and-also[140] with-those after-the-war. I-hope-that-you-will[150]-be-able-to see at-once that all-parts-of[160]-the-world were affected, and your-company did as-well[170]-as any-other.

This-statement showing-the history of-our[180]-company will-be sent to-you within-the-next-few[190]-weeks.                    (191)

(c) *College advertisement*

It-may-well-be that-you have-not heard of[10]-our College, as-we-are not-yet very-well-known.[20] We-can offer-you a service second-to-none in[30]-this-country and, perhaps, in-the-world.

As-will-be[40]-seen from-the prospectus to-be sent-out in-a[50]-few-weeks'-time, boys as-well-as girls are accepted.[60] The work in-the class-room is identical for-all, but[70] games periods out-of-doors are for-the-most-part[80]-conducted separately.

A basic charge-of £500 per[90]-head per-annum will-be-made. To-this will then[100] be added various-charges rated at ten per-cent, five[110] per-cent and two and a half per-cent of[120]-that total. Anything-else is-not costed at so-much[130] per-cent but at so-much per-day.          (138)


(d) *Parliamentary speech*

The Hon.-Member speaking in-the-House-of-Commons said:[10] "The Hon.-Member on-the-other-side-of this-House[20] has-said-that-the Government has-not-been able-to[30] keep down prices, despite-the very strong measures that-were[40] taken to-do-so. At-the-same-time, he-says,[50] wages have-been unable-to rise at anything-like a[60] reasonable rate. If-it-were true, I should-be-the[70] very-first-to-admit it, but it-is-not.

"We[80]-are in-the-same position as a great-many nations[90] in-all-parts-of-the-world. It-would-appear that[100]-the present-state-of trade both at-home-and-abroad[110] is improving, and-we-are doing as-well-as-possible[120] in-the-circumstances." The Hon.-Member said this-was due[130] entirely to-action on-the-part-of our-own-Government[140] and other steps which-were being taken by other-governments[150] through-out-the-world.          (153)


## SELECTED PHRASES 14

1. it-is-connected, we-are-not-connected, in-connection(with), no-connection(with), no-connections, there-is-no-connection, we-have-no-connection, and-connected

2. they-consider-the, unable-to-consider, we-shall-consider-the-matter, it-is-continuous, almost-continuous, in-contact, should-continue, on-the-Continent, several-continents

3. we-cannot-contról, you-will-control, it-is-controlled, we-are-unable-to-control, can-you-control-the, you-should-control, in-control, our-control, and-control

4. in-the-contract, in-their-contract, in-this-contract, your-contract, formal-contract, in-contemplation, what-is-contemplated, greatly-concerned, were-concerned

5. we-cannot-compete, we-must-compete, we-have-competed, you-are-competing, this-competition, your-competition, overseas-competition, ùnfair-competition, in-competition

6. heavily-committed, you-are-committed, would-not-be-committed, many-commitments, we-have-no-commitments, in-committee, if-the-committee, should-the-committee, on-the-committee

---

7. we-must-complete-the, if-he-completes, we-have-completed, it-is-completed, it-has-been-completed, in-completion, we-are-compelled, feel-compelled
8. you-should-compare, if-he-compares, by-comparison, much-more-common, it-is-common-knowledge, is-it-common, minor-complaint, childish-complaint, nervous-complaint
9. income-tax, income-tax-commitments, income-tax-control, income-tax-requirements, income-tax-tables, income-tax-form, income-tax-demand, income-tax-code
10. in-conclusion, come-to-the-conclusion, to-come-to-the-conclusion, we-have-come-to-the-conclusion, we-have-concluded, some-considerable-time, very-considerable-time, take-into-consideration
11. I-considered, I-considered-the-matter, it-is-considered, it-is-to-be-considered, I-consider, you-may-consider, they-may-consider, we-may-consider, in-consequence(of)
12. your-ability, your-abilities, our-ability, our-abilities, their-ability, their-abilities, this-ability, these-abilities, her-ability, her-abilities

---

13. we-have-no-ability, they-have-no-ability, improve-the-ability, cultivate-the-ability, best-abilities, poor-abilities, best-of-my-ability, best-of-your-ability, best-of-our-ability, best-of-their-ability
14. in-reality, no-reality, there-is-no-reality, to-face-reality, can-there-be-reality, it-would-be-logical, you-are-not-logical, it-is-not-logical, if-we-are-logical, they-are-not-logical
15. your-mentality, their-mentality, high-mentality, of-low-mentality, of-this-mentality, of-such-mentality, poor-mentality, undeveloped-mentality, well-developed-mentality
16. this-ship, new-ship, your-ships, our-ships, several-ships, these-ships, for-shipment, poor-shipment, small-shipment, large-shipment
17. some-shipments, fine-shipments, big-shipments, last-shipments, huge-shipments, overseas-shipments, Transatlantic-shipments, delayed-shipments
18. in-the-fullness-of-time, several-yards, dozen-yards, two-yards, we-are-controlling-the-competition, we-shall-complete-the-contract, we-shall-consider-the-consequences

# PRACTICE MATERIAL 14

## (a) *Extract from company report*

You-will-be-concerned to know-that-the-combination of[10] income-tax-requirements and other-commitments beyond our-control have[20] conspired to-make-conditions very difficult indeed for-us during[30]-the past-year. Other-companies with-whom we-are in[40]-competition have-had much-the-same experience. In-the-last[50]-few-months of-the-year, valuable-contracts for large-shipments[60] to-the-Continent were-con-cluded, and-we-must-consider ourselves[70] very-lucky, as-it-would otherwise have-been our worst[80] year for-some-considerable-time. In-consequence-of these-shipments,[90] a small-profit has-been-made, and you-must-consider[100]-the results very-satisfactory in-comparison-with-the loss we[110]-expected.

We-are-now-confident that-we-shall-be-able[120]-to-continue to in-crease our output by about three per[130]-cent per-annum. This-conclu-sion has-been reached after serious[140]-consideration of-our position and-prospects. We-must take-into[150]-consideration the fact that-we-are-unable-to-control-the[160] rate-of-income-tax—and-that-commitment alone is a[170] heavy one. On-the-other-hand, we-have-completed several-contracts[180] and, in-consequence, we-can expect to-receive a[190] very large-sum-of-money shortly. We-have-had no[200]-complaints about-the work, and-the-companies-concerned have asked[210]-us to-keep in-contact with-them. There-is-some[220] suggestion that-the-contracts might be-continued, and it-seems[230]-logical that that-would-be-contemplated. This-would enable-us[240] to-meet overseas-competition, which-has-been-increasing.

In-conclusion,[250] I-now-confirm what-has-been-common-knowledge for-some[260]-time—that-the-directors feel-compelled to discontinue the bonus[270] payment for-this year. In-connection-with-the dividend, they[280]-have-considered-the-matter and-have-come-to-the-conclusion that[290] a small increase might be possible. (297)

## (b) *Letter concerning special schools*

Dear-Madam, We-are-conducting a survey in-connection-with[10]-the provision of-special schools not-only for-those of[20]-low-mentality but also for-those of high-mentality. It[30]-is-not-logical to-give special-attention to-those-who[40]-have an undeveloped-mentality unless-com-parable accommodation is-to-be[50]-considered for-those-who-have a highly developed-mentality. Special[60] schools are-considered necessary for backward children, but it-is[70] very uncommon for-consideration to-be given to youngsters who[80]-are particularly bright.

We-are greatly-concerned about this situation[90] and-feel-compelled to ask-you to help-us. We[100]-are, in-reality, doing no-more-than to ask for[110]-the-same-consideration to-be given to all-those children[120] who-are suffering because of-their-own-abilities or lack[130]-of them. It-would-be-logical to-treat pupils of[140] high-mentality as being just-as unusual as-those-who[150]-are of poor-mentality.

We-are-confident that-you-will[160]-agree to complete-the enclosed-form. Yours-faithfully, (168)

(c) *Parliamentary speech on prices and wages*

The Chancellor-of-the-Exchequer said-that it-was beyond[10]-the-control of-the-Government to compel reductions in prices[20] to-be-made. He-continued: "I-consider that-it-is[30]-time Hon.-Members on-the-other-side of-this-House[40] were-made to-face-reality. They-appear to-con-sider-that[50] we should-control prices at-all-levels. This-is, of[60]-course, impossible when-we-are-completely unaware of-what-is[70]-contemplated by employees, some of-whom have-completed formal-contracts[80] with their employers. If constant demands are made for rises[90] in-the rate-of-pay, employers may-be-compelled to[100]-raise prices. In-addition, the loss of a large-shipment[110] from-the-Continent, due to ill-considered action on-the[120]-part-of some workers, is bound to-cause-complete chaos.[130] In-consequence, many-concerns who-have-had-constant trouble of[140]-this sort are quite unable-to-continue trading." (148)

(d) *Statement to members of trading association*

As secretary of-the Traders'-Association, I-am-compelled to[10] inform-you that-we-cannot-control-the prices charged by[20]-all traders. Those-who-have joined your-association conform to[30]-the suggestions made by-the-committee. Prices are-not-completely[40]-controlled, and-traders are still able-to-compete, but-we[50]-are-concerned about unfair-competi-tion from non-members.

We-shall[60]-continue to-the best-of-our-ability to convince such[70]-competitors to-join with-us, so-that we-may all[80] fight overseas-com-petition together. We-have-come-to-the-conclusion[90] that-this-is more sensible than-considering legal action, which[100]-would take some-considerable-time to-set in motion, and[110]-we-must take-into-con-sideration also the cost of-such[120]-action. We-are-confident that-we-shall-be-able-to[130]-complete a satisfactory-contract with-these traders in a short[140]-time. (141)

## SELECTED PHRASES 15A

1. party-leader, party-manifesto, dinner-party, birthday-party, Pro-fessor-Morris, Chemistry-Professor, works-superintendent, police-superintendent, Superintendent-Williams

2. Bank-of-England, Lloyds-Bank, Barclays-Bank, merchant-bank, river-embankment, Thames-Embankment, bill-of-sale, Private-Member's-Bill, Treasury-bills

3. for-your-attention, draw-your-attention-to-the-fact, your-attention-to-the-matter, how-much-attention, personal-attention, Department-of-Commerce, Commerce-Department, department-stores, Housing-Department, several-departments

4. handling-charge, you-will-be-charged, higher-charges, free-of-charge, in-charge, Chancery-Appeal, Chancery-Judge, journal-entries, house-journal, professional-journal, trade-journal

5. company-auditors, ballet-company, in-your-company, finance-companies, council-chamber, County-Council, council-approval, British-Medical-Council

6. capital-city, capital-letters, issued-capital, issued-capital-of-the-company, capital-expenditure, new-capital, captain-of-the-ship, group-captain, Captain-Brown

---

7. Engineering-Co.-Ltd, Manufacturing-Co.-Ltd, Mercantile-Co.-Ltd, Colonel-Jackson, Colonel-Briggs, corporation-tax, overseas-corporations, Steel-Corporation

8. government-official, local-government, government-orders, United-States-Government, French-Government, parliamentary-government, this-government, of-this-government

9. form-of-agreement, order-form, entry-form, medical-form, it-was-formed, it-will-be-formed, high-valuation, low-valuation, agent's-valuation, probate-valuation

10. local-authority, necessary-authority, several-authorities, very-best-authorities, by-some-authorities, superior-authorities, on-my-authority, higher-authority, supreme-authority

11. few-months, three-or-four-months, several-months-ago, in-this-month, six-months-ago, next-month, three-months, Society-of-Engineers, Building-Society, in-this-society, modern-society

12. high-water-mark, trade-mark, finger-marks, dirty-marks, Major-Thompson, Major-Robinson, major-setback, major-development

---

13. tomorrow-morning, this-morning, yesterday-morning, spring-morning, summer-morning, autumn-morning, winter-morning, morning-session, beautiful-morning

14. National-Giro, foreign-national, national-interests, national-disaster, will-you-enquire, for-your-enquiry, this-enquiry, letter-of-enquiry, police-inquiries, several-enquiries

15. Liberal-Party, liberal-measures, Liberal-leader, liberal-payments, limited-company, limited-knowledge, Caterers-Ltd, Selfridges-Ltd, Carter-Ltd
16. you-can-arrange, will-you-arrange, if-he-may-arrange, it-has-been-arranged, had-you-arranged, previously-arranged, this-arrangement, excellent-arrangement, please-make-arrangements, new-arrangements
17. railway-station, railway-timetable, miniature-railway, mountain-railway, British-Railways-Board, private-railways, do-you-require, if-you-require, you-may-require
18. when-it-is-required, whenever-required, estimated-requirement, further-requirement, substantial-requirements, your-requirements, other-requirements, Conservative-Party, conservative-estimates

## PRACTICE MATERIAL 15A

*Financial negotiations*

The party-leaders of-the three main political-parties have[10]-had a meeting with representatives of-the Bank-of-England[20] at-one-of-the Government-offices on-the Thames-Embankment.[30] The main subject of-discussion was-the effect-of-the[40] Private-Member's-Bill introduced four-or-five-months-ago in[50]-connection-with Treasury-bills and merchant-banks. An article by[60] Professor-Morris in-this-month's Financial-Journal led Superintendent-Williams[70] to-bring-the-matter to-the personal-attention of-the[80] head-of-the appropriate-department of-the-Government. New-arrangements[90] will-be-required to-cover-the matters of national-interest.[100] The question of capital-issues by Carter-Ltd and-the[110] Mercantile-Co.-Ltd, in-view of-the low-valuations, will[120]-be-inquired into, before a Chancery-Appeal is-considered. There[130]-is-also-the matter of liberal-payments to company-directors,[140] and, at a conservative-estimate, the whole-inquiry may last[150] three-months. (152)

## SELECTED PHRASES 15B

1. policy-of-the-Board, insurance-policies, life-policies, government-policy, policy-of-the-Government, Bishop-of-Coventry, Roman-Catholic-Bishop, bring-forth, set-forth
2. scientific-research, scientific-work, scientific-publication, scientific-proof, scientific-staff, scientific-field, to-make-application, form-of-application, formal-application, written-application, for-your-application

3. judicial-punishment, severe-punishment, some-punishment, capital-punishment, business-dealings, new-business, our-business, business-man, business-life, business-relations
4. at-the-beginning, from-the-beginning-to-the-end, in-the-beginning, very-beginning, from-beginning-to-end, is-it-convenient, if-it-is-not-convenient, whenever-convenient, at-your-convenience, early-convenience
5. life-assurance, endowment-assurance, positive-assurance, personal-assurance, similar-letters, similar-results, similar-documents, similar-situation, similar-terms
6. comprehensive-insurance, marine-insurance, fire-insurance, motor-car-insurance, this-insurance, any(-in)-communication, further-communication, for-your-communication, urgent-communication

## PRACTICE MATERIAL 15B

### (a) *Circular-letter from insurance company*

Ladies-and-Gentlemen, A similar-situation to-that which occurred[10] last-year has arisen. It-is-now necessary for-us[20] to-make-application to increase-the rates for insurance-policies[30] of all-kinds. This-will affect-the life-department, in[40]-relation-to endowment-assurance, as-well-as-the other-departments[50] of-our-business dealing-with fire-insurance and other risks.[60] It-has always-been-the policy-of-the-Board from[70]-the very-beginning to-keep you informed of-changes in[80]-the policy-of-the-Government. It-is for-this-reason[90] that-we-are-sending-you this further-communication. We-shall[100] let-you-have particulars of-the detailed changes as-soon[110]-as they-are made available to-us. They-are to[120]-be set-forth in a special document. We-hope that[130]-this will-be-convenient to-you.                     (136)

### (b) *Notice to prison reform committee*

The Bishop-of-Coventry has-been appointed to-the-committee[10] dealing-with prison reform. It-is hoped that-the-members[20] of-the-committee will take-advantage of-the information to[30]-be-found in-some scientific-publications dealing-with capital-punishment,[40] as-this-may-have some-connection with-the-committee's final[50] recommendations on-the approach to judicial-punishment in general. As[60]-is to-be expected, there-are different opinions on-this[70]-subject. Some-people think-that-the effect-of-the trial[80] and-conviction are sufficient-punishment, while others believe-that severe[90]-punishment should follow any crime. The considered-conclusions of-this[100]-committee will-be set-forth in-their report.                     (108)

## SELECTED PHRASES 15C

1. in-pursuance(of), in-pursuance-of-the-policy, speaking-from-memory, no-alternative, your-alternative, in-the-House-of-Commons, to-the-House-of-Commons, if-you-will-kindly, if-you-will-kindly-let-us-have
2. for-this-purpose, for-these-purposes, what-is-your-purpose, sole-purpose, for-your-purpose, for-many-purposes, different-purposes, various-purposes, for-several-purposes
3. vote-of-thanks, North-and-South-America, from-time-immemorial, United-Nations, at-right-angles, best-of-my-recollection, rank-and-file, limited-liability-company, value-added-tax
4. we-have-already, we-have-already-said, we-have-already-seen, we-have-already-been, we-have-already-been-there, I-have-already-sent-you, I-have-already-told-you
5. Royal-Commission, Royal-Academy, Royal-Family, Royal-Charter, Royal-Navy, royal-descent, battle-royal, Princess-Royal, Astronomer-Royal
6. atomic-power-station, atomic-energy, atomic-radiation, atomic-number, atomic-clock, atomic-explosion, atomic-pile, atomic-nucleus, atomic-power

## PRACTICE MATERIAL 15C

*Letter concerning official function*

Dear Sir-James, I-have-already-sent-you details of[10]-the opening of a new atomic-power-station by a[20] member-of-the Royal-Family. To-the best-of-my[30]-recollection, I-told-you also that-it-was expected that[40] at-least one representative of-the United-Nations would-be[50] present, as-well-as some distinguished visitors from North-and[60]-South-America. I very-much hope-that-you-will-not[70]-be-required in-the-House-of-Commons on-that date,[80] as I-would-like-you to-propose-the vote-of[90]-thanks to-our guest speaker at-the dinner-party that[100]-has-been-arranged for-the evening. Speaking-from-memory, no[110]-alternative person has-been chosen in-case you-cannot come,[120] so will-you-kindly let-me-know as-soon-as[130]-possible whether you-will-be free for-this-purpose? Yours,[140]                                         (140)

## SELECTED PHRASES 16A

1. most-important, almost-certain, almost-impossible, last-time, in-your-last-letter, past-year, Post-Office, West-End-of-London, there-is-still

2. take-steps, first-rate, for-the-most-part, next-few-months, just-received, last-week, last-month, most-probable
3. must-be, at-the-last-moment, West-Indian, better-still, past-few-days, very-pleased-indeed, we-are-very-pleased-indeed, enclosed-receipt
4. take-exception, to-take-exception, make-exceptions, break-cover, animal-life, hardly-likely, family-life
5. early-life, political-life, some-measure, in-some-measure, most-important-measure, prime-minister, satisfactory-record, satisfactory-records
6. satisfactory-result, unsatisfactory-results, very-satisfactory-results, poor-results, better-results, satisfactory-reason, zero-rated, you-are-requested, British-ships, machine-shops

---

7. on-the-other-side-of-the, so-many-other, on-the-other, on-the-other-hand, any-other, no-other, no-other-way, much-more, much-more-important
8. very-much-more, so-much-more, how-much-more, to-look-forward, backwards-and-forwards, carry-forward, carrying-forward
9. in-this-direction, Home-Secretary, Under-Secretary, private-secretary, one-thing, between-them, to-one-another, one-way
10. machine-gun, has-been-made, foreign-affairs, foreign-service, once-again, generally-speaking, once-more, in-the-second-place
11. taken-place, General-Secretary, Foreign-Secretary, in-fact, as-a-matter-of-fact, owing-to-the-fact, worth-while, I-hope-there-is, I-hope-you-will
12. at-home, at-home-and-abroad, at-home-and-overseas, long-life, this-week, next-week, it-will-be, she-will-be, very-well, so-well

## PRACTICE MATERIAL 16A

(a) *Extract from chairman's statement*

I-am-very-pleased-indeed to-be-able-to tell[10]-you that-we-have in-some-measure made very-good[20] progress in-the past-year. You-can-see from-the[30] very-satisfactory-results that-this-is so. On-the-other[40]-hand, there-is-still a long-way to-go before[50] we-are-able-to show a satisfactory-record both at[60]-home-and-abroad. We-are taking-steps in-this-direction,[70] and-in-fact one-thing that-has already-been done[80] is-to-make-sure that British-ships are used much[90]-more-than those of any-other country.

In-the-second[100]-place, it-is hardly-likely that-we-shall-have such[110] a small carry-forward as-we-have-had this year.[120] As-a-matter-of-fact, we-have never done so[130]-well as-we-have in-the past-few-months, and[140]-I-hope-that we-can look-forward to-even better[150]-results next year. (153)

(b) *Political speech*

The Prime-Minister said: "In-the-matter of-foreign-affairs,[10] we-have to-balance, on-the-one-hand, what-is[20] most-important for-us at-home and, on-the-other[30]-hand, what-is most-likely to-seem worth-while to[40] any-other country with-whom we-are trading.

"The Foreign[50]-Secretary visited-the West-Indies last-month and-has returned[60] only in-the past-few-days. He-was able-to[70] put-forward a satisfactory-reason for-the action we-took.[80] As-a-matter-of-fact, I-have-just-received a[90] letter from which it-is-clear that no-one is[100] likely to-take-exception to what we-have-done. There[110]-were a number-of interesting-comments from people in-the[120] West-End-of-London last-week, and-the general opinion[130] is-that-we-can look-forward to settled-conditions once[140]-more." (141)

## SELECTED PHRASES 16B

1. we-have-concluded, for-your-consideration, satisfactory-conclusion, in-conclusion, to-consider, I-will-consider, we-are-concerned, I-am-concerned

2. in-consequence(of), evil-consequences, on-the-contrary, fully-considered, cannot-be-considered, I-consider, I-consider-the-matter, for-consideration

3. further-consideration, to-give-consideration, necessary-conclusion, great-expense, great-expenses, large-expense, large-expenses, heavy-expense, heavy-expenses

4. personal-experience, personal-experiences, recent-experience, recent-experiences, practical-experience, long-experience, we-have-experienced

5. very-favourable, more-favourable, shorthand-writer, shorthand-writing, enclose-herewith, to-send-herewith, if-possible, if-it-is-not-possible, as-soon-as-possible, as-early-as-possible

6. as-soon-as-it-is-possible, as-well-as-possible, if-it-is-possible, as-much-as-possible, it-is-not-possible, your-instructions, I-am-instructed, if-you-will-instruct, musical-instrument

---

7. Kingdom-of-the-Netherlands, United-Kingdom, British-Museum, British-manufacture, British-Isles, British-people, British-goods, British-Rail

8. extremely-sorry, distinctly-understood, extremely-regret, in-this-manner, in-the-same-manner, in-like-manner, in-such-a-manner, in-the-manner
9. Act-of-Parliament, Member-of-Parliament, Acts-of-Parliament, Members-of-Parliament, technical-progress, technical-terms, Technical-College, technical-difficulty
10. we-have-no-objection, there-is-no-objection, I-see-no-objection, I-take-no-objection, high-pressure, extreme-pressure, low-pressure, water-pressure, steam-pressure
11. in-reply(to), in-regard(to), we-have-received, in-reply-to-your-letter, as-regards, we-shall-be-glad-to-receive, your-reply, with-regard-to-the, having-regard-to-the
12. Her-Majesty, Her-Majesty-the-Queen, Her-Majesty's-Government, His-Majesty, His Majesty-the-King, His-Majesty's-Government, you-may-also, it-is-also

## PRACTICE MATERIAL 16B

(a) *Letter concerning new Technical College*

Dear Mr-Moss, I-have-received your-instructions with-regard[10]-to-the opening of-the new Technical-College, and-we[20]-shall-arrange a date as-soon-as-possible. However, I[30]-am-concerned about-the heavy-expenses that-would-be incurred[40] under item three in-your-last-letter. In-consequence, I[50]-enclose-herewith what I-think from long-experience in-these[60]-matters will-be a more-favourable scheme. I-am-extremely[70]-sorry if-you-were given-the wrong estimate, but I[80]-distinctly-understood that-you had-been informed of-the position.[90]

I-see-no-objection to asking your local Member-of[100]-Parliament to perform-the opening. On-the-contrary, I-consider[110] that-it-would make a very-favourable impression.

As-regards[120]-the other-matters you-raised, I-shall-have to-give[130]-them further-consideration before I-can reach a satisfactory-conclusion.[140] Yours-sincerely,                                    (142)

(b) *Addressing royalty*

Some of-the-countries in-the-Common-Market are republics.[10] The head-of a republic is-the president. The British[20]-people, of-course, have a monarchy, as do some-other[30] member nations. In-these-cases, the head-of state is[40]-the king or queen. A king is called His-Majesty,[50] and a queen is called Her-Majesty. If both are[60] entitled to-be addressed in-such-a-manner, they-would[70]-be called Their-Majesties. In-the-United-Kingdom, if-you[80]-were in-fact addressing a king or queen, then you[90]-would say "Your-Majesty". After-the first-time, the correct[100]-forms to-use are "Sir" and "Ma'am".                        (107)

## SELECTED PHRASES 16C

1. for-a-time, at-a-loss, half-a-million, as-a-rule, as-a-result, in-a-few-days, for-a-moment, to-a-great-extent, for-a-minute
2. now-and-then, here-and-there, larger-and-larger, first-and-fore-most, over-and-above, more-and-more, ladies-and-gentlemen, Mr-and-Mrs, black-and-white, round-and-round
3. boys-and-girls, men-and-women, again-and-again, up-and-down, over-and-over-again, ways-and-means, rules-and-regulations, part-and-parcel, north-and-south
4. bigger-and-bigger, longer-and-longer, higher-and-higher, tighter-and-tighter, thinner-and-thinner, rougher-and-rougher, thicker-and-thicker, better-and-better, deeper-and-deeper
5. cheaper-and-cheaper, earlier-and-earlier, louder-and-louder, near-er-and-nearer, greater-and-greater, faster-and-faster, slower-and-slower
6. side-by-side, year-by-year, I-have-come-to-the-conclusion, we-have-come-to-the-conclusion, there-have-been, would-have-been, it-would-have-been, seems-to-have-been, must-have-been, it-must-have-been

---

7. bear-in-mind, borne-in-mind, stock-in-trade, cash-in-hand, keep-in-mind, to-take-into-consideration, to-take-into-account, neither-more-nor-less, neither-this-nor-that
8. difference-of-opinion, expression-of-opinion, point-of-view, in-the-form-of, some-of-them, standard-of-living, years-of-age, City-of-London, way-of-life
9. fact-of-the-matter, facts-of-the-case, out-of-the-question, freedom-of-the-press, one-of-the-most, sign-of-the-times, one-or-two, right-or-wrong
10. yes-or-no, whether-or-not, directly-or-indirectly, what-is-the-matter, in-the-circumstances, on-the-subject, in-the-past, in-the-first-instance, in-the-hands(of), for-the-sake(of), in-the-event(of)
11. I-am-sorry-to-say, needless-to-say, in-addition-to-the, with-regard-to-the, that-is-to-say, in-reply-to-the, having-regard(to), ought-to-have-been, come-to-the-conclusion
12. came-to-the-conclusion, your-attention-to-the-matter, up-to-the-present, up-to-the-present-time, call-attention-to-the-matter, in-connection(with), in-connection-with-the, will-you-please, if-you-please

## PRACTICE MATERIAL 16C

(a) *Statement anticipating possible bankruptcy*

Ladies-and-Gentlemen, We-have-had one-of-the-most[10] difficult years that-we-have-experienced. We-must, of-course,[20] take-into-account and bear-in-mind that what-is[30]-the-matter with-this-country is-that, instead-of production[40] becoming better-and-better as wages rise higher-and-higher,[50] there-have-been strikes and delays so-that production is[60] getting slower-and-slower.

The fact-of-the-matter is[70]-that-we-are coming nearer-and-nearer to-closure, though[80] there-are one-or-two hopeful signs here-and-there[90] that-we-may see improvements as-a-result of-certain[100] action by-some of-the men-and-women in-our[110] many plants up-and-down-the country. Some-of-them[120] have given-us their support, but it-is out-of[130]-the question that-we should allow this-state-of-affairs[140] to continue.

We-have-come-to-the-conclusion—and-I[150]-am-sorry-to-say this—that from-your point-of[160]-view it-would-be better in-the-circumstances to file[170] our-own petition in bankruptcy. In-addition-to-the very[180]-low figure-of cash-in-hand, it-must-be borne[190]-in-mind that year-by-year we-have-had many[200]-other difficulties in-connection-with delays in delivery, which-have[210]-been getting longer-and-longer.

No firm decision has-been[220]-made up-to-the-present, but will-you-please give[230] your-attention-to-the-matter. With-regard-to-the present[240]-state-of-things, we-shall-be sending-you various-forms[250] on-which to-suggest ways-and-means-of-dealing-with[260]-the situation in-the-first-instance. In-the-event-of[270] a difference-of-opinion, we-shall-arrange a proper ballot.[280]

(280)

## (b) *Travel agents' leaflet*

Over-and-over-again, people come-to-the-conclusion that[10] if a holiday is-to-be-considered worth-while it[20]-must-be taken abroad. As-a-matter-of-fact, there[30]-are many-places in-the-British-Isles that-we-can[40] recommend for-your-consideration.

We-take-the-opportunity to-send[50]-herewith our brochure "Special Tours of-Great-Britain". You-will[60]-see that-it-is-possible-to-use your-own car[70] or to-send it a few-days in-advance by[80] British-Rail. It-is-also possible to hire a vehicle,[90] if-that-is more-convenient.

We-shall-be-glad-to[100]-receive your-instructions in-due-course. (106)

## SELECTED PHRASES 17

1. for-the-record, off-the-record, you-can-say, you-can-see, we-do-not, we-don't, with-this, for-those, to-these
2. I-know, we-know-that, it-may-seem, who-can-be, it-is-unnecessary, it-is-unnatural, it-is-unknown, we-are-unable-to
3. in-all-cases, for-the-year, very-well, I-expected, we-inspected, I-represented, we-informed, I-objected

4. I-regard, I-regret, my-own, in-my-own-way, in-many-ways, in-the-course-of-time, in-course-of-time
5. if-there-is(-has), for-there-is(-has), if-it, for-it, in-other-ways, any-other-ways, large-part(of), large-number-of, very-much, in-a-position, unable-to
6. we-are, we're, you-are, you're, they-will, they'll, I-am, I'm, I-will, I'll

## PRACTICE MATERIAL 17

### (a) *Comments on annual accounts*

You-will note with pleasure that-the-profit for-the[10]-year is much higher-than-the profit made in-the[20] year before. It-is-not necessary for-me to-go[30] into great detail here regarding-the accounts, but it-can[40]-be-seen that-we-have in-all-cases done better[50]-than we-expected. I-regret-that-the accounts reached-you[60] rather later-than usual, but-you all know-the reason,[70] and it-is-unnecessary to-repeat it here. You-will[80]-see from-the figures that-we-have-done very-well,[90] despite-the cancellation of very large orders in two-cases.[100] In-the-circumstances, we-expected to-lose some-business, but[110]-we-did-not-think-the loss would-be of-those[120] particular accounts. (122)

### (b) *Memorandum*

I-regret-to-say that-this work is by-no[10]-means-complete. My-own part is ready, and-I-am[20] in-a-position to-let-you-have it at-once.[30] However, it-is-unnecessary to-remind you that Mr-Brown[40] has-been very ill. Strictly off-the-record, it-seems[50]-likely that some-other-arrangements will-have to-be-made[60] with-regard-to-the part-of-the work that-you[70] gave to-him. Mr-Brown has told-me that-the[80] doctors expect it to-be at-least six-months before[90] they-will let-him return home. In-the-circum-stances, if[100]-there-is-anything I-can-do, please-let-me-know.[110] I-know of a large-number-of young-men who[120]-would-be-able between-them to complete-the work in[130]-the-course-of-time. It-is-possible that I might[140] be-able-to do a large-part-of-the work[150] myself, but I-am-unable-to-commit myself at-this[160]-time. (161)

## SELECTED PHRASES 18

1. one-or-two, two-or-three, three-or-four, four-or-five, five-or-six, six-or-seven, three, six, eight, ten
2. 300-people, 500-words, 600-plus, 4,000-men, 7,000-times, 8,000,000, 100,000,000, 8,000,000,000

3. £300, £400, £500, £2,000, £3,000, £5,000, £1m, £100m, £8,000m, £900,000m
4. 1642, 1835, 1907, 2001, 1934, 1976, 1743
5. $2\frac{1}{4}$, $3\frac{1}{4}$, $4\frac{1}{4}$, $9\frac{1}{2}$, $8\frac{1}{2}$, $7\frac{1}{2}$, $5\frac{3}{4}$, $6\frac{3}{4}$, $7\frac{3}{4}$
6. 90%, 40%, 3%, $2\frac{1}{4}$%, 5%-pa, $3\frac{1}{2}$%-pa, 7%-pa, 9%-pa

## PRACTICE MATERIAL 18

*Chairman's speech*

The Chairman-said: "Ladies-and-Gentlemen, it-is-now two[10]-or-three-years since-the very-bad times that-we[20]-experienced when-we lost £2m as-a-result[30] of-forward buying. We-have-only-had one other such incident[40] since-we-were established in 1835,[50] and-that-was at-the-beginning of-this-century.[60] In 1907, we-had to-close three[70]-or-four plants and make over 4,000-men redundant.[80]

"We-have-now recovered from our more recent-experiences, though[90] we-have-completely lost 10 large customers in eight countries.[100] At-the-time of-the-difficulties, we-had to-lay[110] off 600-people and keep another 7,000 on[120] short-time. At-the-present-time, our employees number 100,000,[130] which-is an increase of about 30-per[140]-cent. We-have opened two new plants in major cities,[150] and-we-expect to-repay-the bank-loan (which-is[160] at a fixed rate-of-interest of 7%[170]-pa) within-the-next decade.

"You-will-be interested[180] to know-that-the directors have decided to-make a[190] final payment of $7\frac{1}{2}$%. There[200]-have-been two other payments in-the-last six-months,[210] one of $2\frac{1}{4}$% and-the[220] other of $1\frac{3}{4}$%. That makes[230] a total-of $11\frac{1}{2}$% for[240]-the-year. We-suggest a transfer to-reserves of £500,000[250] and-the payment of £500[260] to-the funds-of-the social-club.

"We-hope-you[270]-will-consider-the results as-satisfactory, and-we-can look[280]-forward to-even better-results in-the next year or[290]-two."

(291)

# Index

243